STUDY SENSE

What Memory Research Tells Us About Studying in College

3rd Edition

by

KRISTINA T. KLASSEN, M.S.
JOHN B. KLASSEN, M.A.T.

macmillan learning
curriculum solutions

bedford/st.martin's • hayden-mcneil • w.h. freeman • worth publishers

ISBN 978-0-7380-8915-7

Macmillan Learning Curriculum Solutions
14903 Pilot Drive
Plymouth, MI 48170
www.macmillanlearning.com

Klassen 8915-7 F16

Hayden-McNeil Sustainability

Hayden-McNeil's standard paper stock uses a minimum of 30% post-consumer waste. We offer higher % options by request, including a 100% recycled stock. Additionally, Hayden-McNeil Custom Digital provides authors with the opportunity to convert print products to a digital format. Hayden-McNeil is part of a larger sustainability initiative through Macmillan Learning. Visit http://sustainability.macmillan.com to learn more.

For Dad & Mom

TABLE OF CONTENTS

Introduction – What does it Mean to Learn? 1

Chapter 1 – Developing the Attitude to Learn 7

Chapter 2 – 3 Categories of Study Habits........................... 15

    Habit – Organizing 15

        Action #1 – Actively Focus My Attention 16

        Action #2 – Preview 19

        Action #3 – Always Read With Pencil & Paper 20

        Action #4 – Group Book & Lecture Notes by Topic 22

        Action #5 – Identify Differences Among Concepts 24

        Action #6 – Establish a Clear Break Between Any 2 Subjects... 27

        Action #7 – Make Compare & Contrast Charts 29

        Action #8 – The Art of Asking Questions 30

        Action #9 – Draw & Color-Code Charts & Diagrams 31

        Action #10 – Study for the Type of Exam I Will Take 32

    Habit – Pacing 34

        Action #11 – Read & Review Immediately After Class.... 34

        Action #12 – One Section at a Time & Keep It Short....... 37

        Action #13 – Review Text & Lecture Notes Daily 39

        Action #14 – Get a Good Night's Sleep After Study 40

    Habit – Overlearning 41

        Action # 15 – Make Information Personal 41

        Action # 16 – Self-Test Frequently 42

        Action #17 – Take a Practice Exam 44

        Action #18 – Correct Returned Exams 46

Chapter 3 – A 7-Step Study Plan 49

Chapter 4 – Applications for Different Courses..................... 55

Chapter 5 – Mastering Math.. 61

Chapter 6 – 4 Differences Between High School & College 83

Chapter 7 – Preparing for Courses.. 87

Chapter 8 – Preparing for Exams 93

Chapter 9 – The Importance of Details... 103

Chapter 10 –The End of Test Anxiety 109

Summary & Conclusion 113

Appendix I – 4 Models of Memory 119

Appendix II – Memory Levels, Entry Keys & Testing Requirements 121

Appendix III – Reasons Why Procrastination Kills Memory 123

Appendix IV – 18 Effective Study Actions 125

Appendix V – Requirements for College Quality Work 127

Appendix VI – A 7-Step Study Plan... 129

Acknowledgements 131

References 133

INTRODUCTION
WHAT DOES IT MEAN TO LEARN?

$\mathcal{M}$egan sits in the student lounge staring at her textbook. In an hour she will take a chemistry exam and she is panicked. Even though she has already spent eight hours this week reading over her text and notes, she still cannot seem to grasp the principles that are going to be on the test. With her grade hovering between D and F, she is hoping that somehow she can pull off a C by finals to avoid failing this course that is required for her major.

Up walks Eric, her lab partner. "Hi, Megan. You look worried. What's going on?" As Eric heard Megan describe her dilemma, he could relate to her feelings very well. He knew what would help her because he had come from the same place.

"Meg, I hear you and I understand completely. My first semester in college, it didn't seem to matter how much I read the textbook or went over my notes, I could never seem to do well on tests. In fact, I nearly flunked out at mid-term. "I remember thinking, 'how am I ever going to make it in college?' But I kept trying.

"When I got back a math exam with a 12% score, I finally came to accept the mess I was in. I had run out of options and was desperate to find the answer. I had reached the point that I didn't care anymore that people would find out I didn't know what I was doing.

"That day, as I hopelessly sat staring at my failed test in the campus caféteria, I heard a voice behind me say, 'Can I help you?' I turned around and there stood my math instructor, and all I could manage was, "I don't think it is possible for me to make it in college, I've tried everything."

"In a compassionate voice, he said, 'Son, if you follow all that I tell you, you will never, ever worry about your grades again.'

"Right then and there I grabbed onto that lifeline. Ever since, I have faithfully followed the advice my instructor gave me, and that has made all the difference. He gave me the key that unlocked and stimulated an area deep inside me I never knew existed. Grades are no longer the issue."

"I can see that. You don't seem to be at all worried about the test today. What was the instructor's advice to you?"

"It was actually very simple. He said that because we become what we give our attention to, I had to focus on mastering everything in the course rather than focus on the grade. Then, he gave me specific steps to follow. Frankly, I was terrified. Looking to master my courses and not worrying about grades felt like jumping off a bridge into nowhere, but the result was amazing. It landed me in the most comfortable place ever. I was astounded that I not only ended up with straight As in all of my courses, but overall, I spent less time and learning has actually become fun."

"I don't know how to do that."

"I know. I didn't either. I didn't come into the world with a natural attitude to listen to someone else. In fact, the very opposite was true. I thought I knew it all. But I realized that I had to make a decision. Do I commit myself and everything I am to listening to my instructor or remain in my old habits and just work for a grade?

"In my previous experience, 'learning' had meant repetitious memorizing and producing raw answers that gave an impression that I understood what I was doing. Yet, over the long run, I discovered that none of it guaranteed I learned anything and my grades reflected that. It certainly did not transfer to the next course I had to take.

"Deeply mastering a concept to the point where I can fully explain it in detail requires me to have an entirely different focus than I ever thought was part of academics. This depth produces complete, lasting answers to all questions I can be asked. It surprised me that I was so caught up in mastering the material I completely forgot about the grades, yet they were there.

"Although you feel like you don't know how to succeed in school, you already have the power within you, released when you actively search for meaning. By asking the question, 'how can I do this?' you have taken the first step in seeking to discover the answer. You are is primed for learning, and that always pays off.

"You see, Meg, I found that study is not merely mechanics. In my search for success, I discovered that my old attitude toward learning was a product of wrong habits formed by my wrong approach based on repetitious actions like memorizing only to regurgitate without understanding. That is what needed to change.

"To listen intently and take instruction became my new foundation for learning, since all education comes from listening to and obeying instructions given by a master of the subject, who was put there to teach (otherwise, I would not need school at all). The mechanics of what to do is secondary; they are just that the mechanics, and they certainly help me become more efficient, but without comprehension, they don't provide satisfaction and success in learning. This new attitude and its efficient mechanics not only go hand-in-hand towards success, they are success in themselves.

"My old attitude was to only follow the raw mechanics of memory and ignore the most important requirement: a teachable, open, active mind seeking to learn to the point of mastering entire concepts. Although the correct answer may have given a surface illusion that I knew something, that really didn't last very long and I came away feeling empty.

"Research in psychology shows that it doesn't matter how much I think I want to learn material, how much effort I put in, how hard a course is, or how much time I spend on it. When I approach the material with an actively submissive mind (because learning is to submit) and free the brain to work the way it was made, then I master it.

"In other words, the most important factor involved in mastering our chemistry course is the dynamics of our new attitude in order to make the process of learning successful. This is constructed by the mechanics of correct repetitious actions forming correct and powerful habits of successful life and learning.

"It does not depend on sincerity, course difficulty, effort or time. Certainly, I must intend to learn, want to learn, spend time and review, but these alone do not guarantee that I will remember. If that is all I do, I would still find myself frustrated and not understanding what I was doing. Full mastery is totally under my control and can be accomplished by anyone with this attitude."

Megan listened intently. She had never considered how critical her attitude was for her success. And she is not alone.

The little book you are about to read maps out a plan for anyone and everyone to succeed in academics at all levels. We wrote this book for you because years ago we found ourselves in the exact same situation as Meg and Eric faced: needing to master the often scary mystery of academic success.

This is what Eric's instructor laid out for him and is based on countless hours spent in research to discover the biological principles of how memory works, from why a student's attitude is important to specific study actions.

Please enjoy the book and the academic challenges ahead. They are yours to master because the key to learning resides within you. You will find the results amazing.

All the best to you,
John & Kristina

Actions ⇨ Habits ⇨ Attitude

CHAPTER 1
DEVELOPING THE ATTITUDE TO LEARN

My attitude toward learning is the single most powerful element in my academic success. It determines my focus, it defines my goal, it directs all of my activities. It dictates whether or not I remember anything at all.

What is attitude? How can I develop a proper attitude to learn? It all begins with effective action, which means actions that work, and study actions based on how I form memories always work. I cannot change my attitude without changing my actions, because actions that I repeat form habits and habits that I continually engage

**ACTIONS ⇨
HABITS ⇨
ATTITUDE**

in form attitudes. Overall, my attitudes determine my destiny in life.

This means that as I regularly follow the actions that generate lasting memories, I form a learning habit that gives me an attitude primed for success. In the end, I become addicted to learning, addicted to success because it has become part of the very fabric of my being and determines my future. This is powerful.

MY FOCUS

Focus is concentration and direction. What I focus on directs my actions and shapes my habits.

**MY FOCUS
DIRECTS MY
ACTIONS**

What is my view of learning? When I focus on grades and the "golden GPA" I hear constantly emphasized, I view learning as compartmentalized activity, mechanics and study techniques to memorize details which are soon forgotten after the course ends. But when I focus on understanding, I view learning as continuously building solid distinctions about entire concepts that stay with me for the rest of my life.

I fulfill whatever goal I have.

ELIMINATING FEAR

A proper attitude also eliminates the fear generated by slavery to grades. While exams and grades provide necessary motivation for my actions, *focusing* on grades themselves without identifying the actions required to achieve them makes them appear to be beyond control. This can turn normal "performance anxiety" into terror.

> **FOCUSING ON GRADES GENERATES FEAR**

On the other hand, focusing on full understanding and mastery of all course concepts is tangible and completely within my control. It is not scary or elusive at all. I can do simple, efficient things to make sure that I understand completely, and the results are amazing.

A goal of full mastery of any and all course material ensures that I have a solid foundation for life and career *as well as* the grades I need. "GPA" comes to mean "Generated Proper Attitude."

> **"GPA" = GENERATED PROPER ATTITUDE**

The question is, "How do I get there? Doesn't developing complete understanding take a lot of time? My time is limited with work, school, social life and family."

The surprising answer to this question is that it really does not take more time at all. Actually, it takes *less*. The difference is proper focus + efficiency. It is a researched fact that the most successful students spend *less* time studying than those who fail. When my focus is set to master material *and* I know how to work efficiently, the rest is automatic.

> **MASTERY TAKES *LESS* TIME**

MY GOAL

My attitude sets my goal and *only an active, involved mind can learn.* Therefore, my goal, my entire focus and mind-set must be on full mastery of all course material.

> **DIFFERENCE BETWEEN UNDERSTANDING & RECOGNITION**

Recognition and understanding for mastery are 2 separate functional steps. Although I can read through a book or listen in class and *recognize* ideas, this doesn't mean I have *understood the words in context.* Recognition is only the first step. Understanding is the arrival.

There are three important reasons why a focused, active mind is necessary for mastery. First, research tells me that I *only* generate the brain waves *required* for long-term memory when I am actively focused on understanding. Memories are only set when I generate the specific patterns formed by evaluating new material and deciding what is important, grouping information, seeking answers and asking questions. I can't argue with pure biology. To be passively involved (only surface reading through a textbook or mindless copying) will not work.

> **ACTIVE MIND = NECESSARY BRAIN WAVES**

If I am not generating these specific waves, the brain doesn't *keep* the information, just like I discard a banana peel or sort through the mail and keep only what I need. I only remember what is important.

For example, when I read over unfamiliar material, I only relate to the general idea of a topic, focusing on the nouns (I am asking, "what is this about?"). But if I were promised $1,000,000 to discover and explain the core idea behind a paragraph, I would be actively focused and never forget what it said.

Only an active mind sets lasting memories.

On the other hand, a passive, unengaged mind lets everything drift by. I may identify it all, but nothing sticks. So, reading a textbook with a passive mind (just reading to recognize individual words) is like watching

NOTHING
STICKS TO A
PASSIVE MIND

a river flow by, enjoying the scene and recognizing that fish are swimming in it but never reaching in to grab one for lunch. I have spent time looking at it and recognize that it is a river but take nothing away for later use.

Second, no learning takes place without a listening, submitted mind, committed to taking instruction and doing every task my instructor requires. Without actively taking instruction, I am just "jumping through the hoops," not really learning anything. But with an active mind, set to listen and follow direction, course material becomes an integral part of me and is easy to recall whenever I need it.

LEARNING
REQUIRES
LISTENING

Third, my goal sets the "filter" to only keep the incoming data I will need. For example, if I "read pages 345-397," my eyes will move back and forth over the pages and at the end I will be lucky to only remember the major topic. Because the goal was to get through the pages, that is what I did. However, when the goal is to understand, organize and explain the information, I seek out major ideas and put them together as I read. I only remember information *in the way I attend to it.*

Ryan, Brandon and Matt are roommates. They are in their first year at Grand State University and went to high school together. All scored approximately the same on the SAT, about average for entering freshmen. All three are in the same courses, looking toward engineering degrees.

Every morning at 7 a.m., Ryan wakes up and groans to himself, "Do I really have to go to class today?" He is particularly tired since he stayed up until 2 a.m. playing video games.

He spends the first 10 minutes of his day in bed, trying to think of ways he can get around attending his 8 a.m. physics class. Here are some of his regular morning thoughts:

1. I'll learn more if I just get the notes from Matt, because I'll only fall asleep in class.

2. I will be more rested to study later if I stay in bed one more hour.

3. Professor Vector doesn't count attendance, so he'll never miss me.

4. If I ace my higher level courses, this Introduction to Physics course won't count very much when I go to transfer to engineering school.

Needless to say, Ryan only goes to class when he thinks he absolutely has to. When he is there, he sits in the back of the room and text-messages his friends, only paying attention when the instructor raises his voice or writes something on the board. He copies down exactly what the teacher says or writes. At home, he reads the first paragraph of his textbook and scans the rest. He does barely enough to meet the basic course requirements.

At exam time, Ryan looks through his notes once, the first time he has read them since the lecture. "I'll be okay," he reasons, " I understand this." At midterm, Ryan is surprised to find an F for his physics grade. Is he mad! "Boy, Prof. V is really unfair! I did everything he required!"

Ryan had never decided to listen to anybody. He had only done what felt good to him at the time in order to somehow get a grade. His passive attitude was formed from bad study *habits*, themselves formed from wrong study *actions*. The attitude, "Is this good enough?" never works.

Brandon has the same physics course. He is trying "as hard as he can" to get an A. Every morning at 7 he is up and ready for school, but is sometimes late because he isn't very organized. He attends class regularly, pays attention and takes notes. Before exams, he reviews his notes and textbook. He even reads late into the night to make sure that he is never behind in his course material. But at midterm, Brandon gets a C in physics. He goes home dejected. As he enters the apartment he tells his roommates, "Boy, college sure is hard! I studied hours for this course but I can never get higher than a C+, and I only got that once. I have no more time I can spend. I guess I am not smart enough to get As."

An attitude that says, "I'm trying as hard as I can," doesn't get top grades, either.

I have to be careful of the word "try." "Try" means that I have done all I could without becoming actively involved. It is a passive attitude because I reject my responsibility. It is both a false justification for my failure and a condemnation of my instructor or someone else. "I tried" = "I" have done everything "I" could, so either I don't have the ability or someone else made it too hard.

If it doesn't work, it's not my fault. It is an excuse for not developing the study habits that build an active, successful attitude.

Matt is also in that physics course. None of his relatives ever graduated from college and only one uncle ever graduated from high school. But Matt set out to fully understand every concept in the course. Full mastery was his top priority. He made it a habit to discover and target all course requirements thoroughly and systematically. Everything he did was focused around organization and understanding.

On Sunday night he would look at his assignment calendar and notice what topics he would be studying in all of his courses that week. Then he took 10 minutes or so and flipped through his textbooks, glancing over the pages that were assigned and making brief "chapter maps" on paper to help build a background for lectures. After that, he packed his book bag for the next day and got a good night's rest so he could process the previews he had developed and be ready for class. In the morning he was always relaxed and arrived early. He consistently sat in the same seat in the front row because he said this kept him from being distracted.

During Prof. Vector's lecture he kept eye contact with him, listening to understand how the professor was thinking and what steps he was explaining. He listened intently, following along with the instructor's reasoning and only writing down questions. Then, after Physics, while he was waiting for English class to begin, he read over the questions and thought them through for later when he had a chance to discover the answers. He knew that if he didn't, he would forget them. It was always easier when he did this.

Later that same night, Matt filled in the chapter map as he read the textbook, being sure to read only one section at a time and take breaks between them. He looked up his questions, making notes when he found parts that he didn't understand. The next day, he went to Prof. V and asked the questions he could not figure out. As a result, he began to understand how Prof. V approached the problems and this made it even easier to understand him in class. He had mapped out the course material so he could visualize it, thought it through to master it, and was careful not to procrastinate on the assignments, which helped to understand it even more.

Matt asked Prof. V what type of tests he gave to aim his study at the proper target. He also regularly explained the course material to another student in class to make sure he understood it. He regularly answered review questions at the end of the chapter. At exam time, he made up a practice test and took it with a timer to make sure he could answer all questions within the time limit. He looked up the answers to questions he was not sure of and repeated the test again until he got it right. After the exam, when his test was returned, he corrected all wrong answers.

At midterm, Matt got the highest grade in the class. He was surprised and very grateful.

The only successful attitude is, "I will master this." My priorities determine my successes.

So, if I catch myself saying, "Is this good enough?" or "I'm trying as hard as I can," that will explain why I am not getting the grades I need. Without the attitude to master all course material, I cannot hope to succeed.

> **RULE OF THUMB**
> **"IS THIS GOOD ENOUGH?" = "D"s or "F"s**
> **"I'M TRYING AS HARD AS I CAN." = "B"s or "C"s**
> **"I WILL FULLY MASTER THIS." = CONSISTENT "A"s**

To change my success, change my attitude. To change my attitude, change my habits. To develop habits that work, I repeat actions that follow the principles of how *memories are stored*. This is where using proper mechanics comes in.

CHAPTER 2
3 CATEGORIES OF STUDY HABITS

I can't argue with biology. Any study action that follows the principles of memory will generate success and any that does not is doomed to fail. It is that simple.

These principles dictate actions that build a *structure* which allows me to learn and make the most efficient use of my time. Even a structure built of inferior material will build a better palace than a disorganized pile of the finest mahogany lumber. Memory requires structure.

All principles of human memory can be grouped into 3 successful study habits: organizing, pacing and overlearning.

Repeated actions form habits. There are 18 specific actions that develop these habits. These actions are based on data from countless hours of memory research which show that it is *what I do* with new information that determines retention.

Habit - ORGANIZING

Only an organized mind can learn. Because the brain is like a filing cabinet, I set up a filing system so I can find stuff whenever I need it. Organization is critical because research shows that I discard whatever is not clear like I do "junk mail." W*hat I actively do* with new information determines whether or not I remember it at all.

> **ONLY AN ORGANIZED MIND CAN LEARN**

Because the entire process of study is the sum total of *all* actions in which I engage to organize course material, it begins right from the moment I enroll in a course.

Study is looking over the course description to see what is included. Study is reading the syllabus. Study is actively listening in class. Study is reading my textbook. Study

> **STUDY IS THE ENTIRE PROCESS**

is outlining the material for myself. Study is sleeping to sort and store everything I worked on the day before. Study is going over my notes to refine them. Study is testing to make sure that I fully understand.

Reading over the course description and syllabus constructs a context for lectures and reading; listening in class, reading the textbook and outlining the information fill in the blanks; asking questions and self-testing refine my understanding; sleeping knits all of the information together into a cohesive picture.

ACTION #1 = ACTIVELY FOCUS MY ATTENTION
RESEARCH PRINCIPLE: *SELECTIVE ATTENTION*

Have you ever noticed something by the side of the road that your friend did not see? What research calls *selective attention* is like a narrow doorway that only lets one item in at a time. Only what I pay attention to is what gets through the door. Research found that the most important part of encoding new information is the ability to ignore irrelevant information. The ability to filter incoming data from the environment decides what is important and worth keeping.

> **PRIORITIES DETERMINE ATTENTION**

It is a matter of priorities. Whatever I consider important gains access and the rest is filtered out. I control what information enters by directing my priorities (this is called "mental set"). If the priority is to organize and explain, I lay the groundwork for learning.

It is a fallacy that I can pay focused attention to more than one thing at once. This is like two or three people trying to barge through a narrow door together. It just doesn't work; only one at a time can pass. This is why distractions are so devastating to study, both in class and while doing homework.

Research shows that *the human brain can only make one conscious decision at a time*, including deciding what to focus on. All decisions occur in the brain region called the "central executive," and anything that

> **I CAN ONLY MAKE ONE DECISION AT A TIME**

demands focus prevents me from attending to course material effectively. (This is exactly why there are 4 times more automobile collisions when drivers are talking on cell phones and 10 times when texting.)

> **FOCUSED ATTENTION = IN-CLASS STUDY**

Because focusing my attention in class is the primary way to collect information, focused attention is in-class study. Therefore, I eliminate all distractions in class as well as when doing homework.

Distractions may be the cell phone, the computer, TV, noise, food, other people, the surroundings, an uncomfortable chair, etc. Whatever it is, I eliminate all distractions as much as humanly possible.

What is wrong with this picture?

> *Larry sits in the back row during English Literature, looking at the girl in front of him. Her hair reminds him of his sister back home, so he pulls out his cell phone and checks his Facebook account to see if she has sent him a message since this morning. Meanwhile, Dr. Bard has been explaining the background behind "The Tempest" that was assigned for the week. 10 minutes later, when Larry finally begins to focus on what Dr. B is saying, he has no clue what is going on. When he begins to read later that day, the play makes no sense to him and he finds himself spending extra time in the library looking up background information on his own, which does not come close to the big picture Dr. B had put together and on which he would be tested.*

CONTEXT HOLDS DETAILS

Larry missed the most important part of what class is all about: providing a context for course information. Without context, details can't hold together. His lack of focused attention blocked the entire learning process. Because instructors spend many hours preparing meaningful context for their students, no amount of home study can ever replace their effort.

What is wrong with this second picture?

> Jessica is studying for a big anatomy test. She is sitting at the dining room table of her apartment with books spread out. Her roommate is cooking dinner while she watches TV in the kitchen. In the living room, the stereo is pounding out music and a party is going on upstairs. She reads a paragraph over four times and closes the book, frustrated. She tells her roommate, "I guess I must be stupid. I just can't seem to understand anatomy."

There is nothing wrong with Jessica. She may feel frustrated, but this is to be expected. Because her senses are taking in so much information at once, her capacity to attend to anatomy is blocked by all of the external distractions. She simply needs to find a quiet place to work, choose a time when not so much is going on around her, turn off the stereo, or do *whatever is needed* for attention to be focused on anatomy.

If I don't minimize distractions and interruptions, I never have a chance to attend to course material. It isn't necessary to have hours and hours that are quiet and uninterrupted. I simply establish a place where I can focus completely for between 15-20 minutes at a time. (More about why 15-20 minutes later on.)

ACTION #2 = PREVIEW
RESEARCH PRINCIPLE: *PRIMING*

Because I store and remember details *only when they fit within a context I already know*, I establish a context before I read a textbook or go to class.

PREVIEWING ESTABLISHES A CONTEXT FOR LEARNING

This looking ahead is called "previewing," which is based on the research principle of priming. When I preview, I don't forget information I spent hours reading and what I heard in lecture during class.

Every time I direct attention toward course topics ahead of time, I am previewing. Choosing the subjects I take determines what general "files" to set up. Looking at the course syllabi tells me what specific topics the courses will cover. Taking 5 minutes to look through the textbook before I read and looking ahead at the day's topic before class primes me to gather new details in the right places. I read over the glossary terms and math formulas even though I don't know what they mean.

At this point, understanding them doesn't matter. It is only important that I have seen them once and know that I will fill in the details later. I have constructed a mental map to be filled in when I get to class and later on read the chapter details. Without previewing, I only remember the general subject after reading for many hours. It makes perfect sense to take 5 minutes instead of 2 hours and accomplish the exact same thing.

When I preview *the day before* class and sleep on it, I automatically form a structure for the next day's work.

SLEEP SETS STRUCTURE

ACTION #3 = ALWAYS READ WITH PENCIL & PAPER
RESEARCH PRINCIPLE: *PRIMACY EFFECT*

Research shows that I remember things the way I *first* interpret them, using my first impression as a base and adding details as I become more familiar. This is known as the "primacy effect."

Students who write down organized notes as they read recall it far

ORGANIZE AS I READ

better later on. When they organize the *first time* they see information, they remember 80% of it, and remember only 20% when they don't.

This is one of the most powerful techniques to gain understanding from textbooks because I use my first impression as a base and add details as I become more familiar. Also, writing information down takes it from the brain's sensory areas (visual & auditory) and deposits it into the thinking areas in the front.

I cannot expect to remember any information if all I do is just read it. The first time I read anything, I relate it to a frame of reference. Then, I go back and clarify information *after* the first reading. It's like moving into a new home and throwing everything into a pile to be sorted out later.

IT IS IMPOSSIBLE TO REMEMBER WHAT I MERELY READ

Imagine how much time I would save if I put every new load into its proper place *as soon as I bring it in.*

Organizing immediately also contributes to distinctiveness because I have never encoded that information in a disorganized form. I take organized notes as I read a chapter the first time, just like I nail down a tarp in a windstorm to keep it from blowing away.

Any way I organize will do just fine, and mine will not be the same as anyone else's. One example of a quick and easy form to make is a "Chapter Map" (Figure 1).

AMERICAN GOVERNMENT - CHAPTER 5: CONGRESS			
REPRESENTATION	**ORGANIZATION**	**LAWMAKING**	**DECISION PROCESS**
Representation *constituency* *delegates* *trustees* *agency representation*	**Cooperation** *institutionalization*	**Committee Deliberation** *open rule* *closed rule*	**Constituency**
Differences Between House & Senate *bicameral legislature*	**Balancing Influence & Interests** *policy implementation* *policy formulation* **Party Leadership** *party caucus* *Speaker of the House* *majority leader* *minority leader* *whip*	**Debate** *extraordinary majority* *filibuster* *cloture* **Presidential Action** *pocket veto*	**Interest Groups** **Party Discipline** *party vote* *roll-call vote* *committee assignments* *access to the floor* *whip system* *logrolling*
The Electoral System *incumbency* *professional legislature* *patronage* *congressional districts* *Gerrymandering*	**The Committee System** *standing committee* *jurisdiction* *gatekeeping authority* *proposal power* *after-the-fact authority* *conference committee* *oversight*	**Distributive Tendency** *policy authorization* *appropriations*	

Figure 1

Making a "Chapter Map"

1. Flip through a textbook chapter and notice how many sections or divisions are in it.

2. Take a horizontal piece of notebook paper and make a column for each division, copying the division titles at the top of each column. Using only a single page records the topic as a single image. More than one page is confusing because the brain forms a new impression for every page separately.

3. Observe how many sub-sections are in each division. For example, in this chapter there are 3 sub-sections under the first major heading, 4 in the second, etc. (usually they are all distinguished by the same font size and/or color in the textbook).

4. Divide the columns with horizontal lines and jot down just the titles of the sub-sections in the appropriate box.

5. List the glossary words that are written in bold or colored text under each section where they appear.

I now have a single, structured breakdown of what I will be reading. As I go on and fill in each section, I am "filing" individual data and easily see how it relates together.

ACTION #4 = GROUP BOOK & LECTURE NOTES BY TOPIC
RESEARCH PRINCIPLE: *CHUNKING*

Oh yes! I understand this subject quite well. I read it over and it really makes sense. But this is only the beginning of the process. If I have only read the material, I have not organized anything.

> *Emily read her notes over 3 times before her political science test and was relaxed and happy. She was confident because she understood all of the ideas. As the tests were passed out and she looked at the page, her heart stopped. She didn't recognize most of the questions!*
>
> *She had never constructed anything that would help her understand and remember the core concepts. It was as if the instructor had passed out a test for the wrong course. Anxiety rose, memory evaporated and she failed miserably.*

Emily never thought about the information in any other way than a group of loose details. She had read over her text and notes, but she had never grouped details together for meaning or integrated her notes with the textbook information. She had not developed a mastery of the ideas. Furthermore, she had not asked what type of questions would appear on the exam to direct her study accordingly and never tested herself on the material. So, it really threw her when the exam questions required her to know more than glossary definitions.

Just recognizing terms or remembering individual facts is not enough when it comes to

COLLEGE LEVEL STUDY = A SHIFT FROM FACTS TO MASTERY

college testing. This shift in the required level of comprehension is one of the main differences between high school and college. (Please see Chapter 6 – 4 Differences Between High School and College.)

To build a cohesive picture, I first need to see which information relates together. Even though very simple, the task of grouping by meaning transforms me from a mere, passive consumer of textbook data into an active thinker and generates brain waves required to set memories.

> **I REMEMBER *CHUNKS* OF INFORMATION**

Grouping also stores information as larger *chunks*. What research calls a "chunk" is any meaningful unit of information based upon experience with similar material.

Research found that the strongest relationship between study time and high test scores is when students spend their time organizing course content. Grouping new information by topic automatically multiplies the ability to remember more material because facts and ideas are stored by topic to be recalled as complete units. Instead of having to remember isolated data, I am now able to access many facts and relationships by recalling one simple category.

> **ONE CATEGORY HOLDS MANY FACTS**

For example, it is easy to read the fact that Henry VIII had six wives. But, group the six different ladies with the dates of their marriage, their countries of birth, their religions and the years of Henry's reign, and a fascinating picture of the political and religious history of Europe emerges.

By grouping for meaning, I can think through different questions and build richer ideas based on that information. Also, dates and facts now fall into place as I recall relationships because memory for the supporting details is almost automatic. I opened the "Henry VIII" file and found what was stored inside.

> *Manuel went to Sociology 101 on Monday after previewing the chapter. That afternoon, he sat at his desk and took notes as he read the text pages on the same material. As he put his book and lecture notes together, he developed a more complete picture of the topic for himself.*
>
> *Tuesday, although he didn't have class, he reviewed all of his notes and jotted down some distinctions between ideas that were similar to see how they related. After class Wednesday he repeated the process of merging text and lecture and Thursday he reviewed all notes to date and wrote down further distinctions between concepts.*
>
> *By repeating this process daily over the two-week period between exams, and explaining it on paper without referring to his text or notes to make sure he had it right, he ended up with a complete, clear picture of the topic and was able to easily recall all of the facts, names, dates, principles and other necessary information to answer all of the exam questions. He had studied successfully.*

When I do what Manuel did, it is actually hard to stop from asking questions and looking deeper into the subject. I am organizing, I am chunking, I am sorting and storing information by category. I am *developing meaning which leads me to fully master* the subject.

ACTION #5 = IDENTIFY DIFFERENCES AMONG CONCEPTS
RESEARCH PRINCIPLE: *DISTINCTIVENESS*

TO REMEMBER SOMETHING, IT *MUST* BE CLEAR

Clarity is critical for memory. Research shows that *anything not distinct (unclear) is not remembered*. That is why this action is so powerful. By recognizing differences, it is easy to distinguish among concepts and build a picture of the material. In order for something to be distinct, it must be clear, which means organized.

The whole process of focused organization *only* works when it produces

DISTINCTIVENESS = PERFECT RECALL

distinctiveness. Making information clear and distinct produces virtually *perfect* recall of details, particularly when I understand the relationships between the ideas. In other words, grouping similar information together and understanding the differences between concepts builds a picture I can retain and use.

> *Justin looked at his history exam, puzzled. He read the essay question over three times. He knew he had read something about the dynasties in ancient China, but he couldn't remember their prominent characteristics or how they were different from each other. If his teacher had simply asked names and dates, he was all right, because he had memorized those, but had not focused on understanding what elements they shared and what made them different from each other.*

Needless to say, Justin is not alone. We have all felt frustrated whenever we have not mastered course information that is required.

College-level thinking and testing require full mastery of all course concepts. When I organize information to clearly understand the concepts and how they are similar and different, I am ready for any type of exam question.

COLLEGE-LEVEL THINKING = UNDERSTANDING CONCEPTS & RELATIONSHIPS

Basic differentiation can be done in many ways. Ian, the engineer, makes flow charts or hierarchies of the core concepts. Li, the art student, draws pictures and color-codes major topics as she underlines her text and class notes. Shea, the English major, likes to make charts of similar words and ideas as she organizes them into categories. Darnell, the pre-med student, reconstructs the text author's outline on paper as he reads. Because they all develop distinctiveness, all will work just fine.

One simple way to differentiate is to make a simple "T" chart and organize the characteristics of different terms or ideas in different columns (Figure 2). I group facts and ideas together to identify general principles of relationship between them.

Psychology 101: Classical vs. Operant Conditioning

	CLASSICAL CONDITIONING	OPERANT CONDITIONING
Behavior:	PASSIVE	ACTIVE
Controlling Stimulus:	BEFORE	AFTER
Generalization?	YES	YES
Discrimination?	YES	YES

Figure 2

Because each person relates to material differently, there is no single way to do this. One student who scored highest in the U. S. on a national electronics test did not relate well to traditional outlines. His test scores improved and his frustration level declined dramatically after he began writing the lecture notes and text organization as a hierarchy (like an electronics diagram-Figure 3), with which he was more familiar.

WE ALL ORGANIZE DIFFERENTLY

There is nothing special about traditional outlines. They are simply one way to communicate the relationship between ideas, and any alternative method to develop distinct pictures will work just as well.

SOCIOLOGY 101

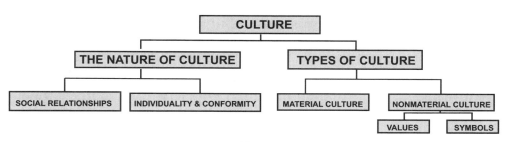

Figure 3

Also, everyone remembers color automatically (research calls this "automatic memory"). If I add a color code to the boxes in the diagram, I have an even more powerful visual representation of large amounts of material at a glance.

ACTION #6 = ESTABLISH A CLEAR BREAK BETWEEN ANY 2 SUBJECTS

RESEARCH PRINCIPLE: *INTERFERENCE*

Dan is sitting in philosophy class thinking that he will never forget what Prof. Premise just said. It makes sense to him, but he does not listen attentively to follow along with the reasoning. When class ends, he gets up and walks across campus to his English literature class and passively listens there, too. After English class, he sits down and opens his books. As he tries to remember what both teachers were talking about, he can't remember any of it in its context. It is all like mud.

Shaking his head in frustration, he closes his books and gives up. Even this little amount of interference made it hard for him to recall what Prof. P said. Because he did not actively attend to either lecture, he did not remember either one successfully.

Because of what researchers call "interference"it takes thoughtful effort to distinguish between what was said in each back-to-back class. This is a bigger problem if they involve similar information, like two different languages or psychology and sociology. Why?

REVIEW & PREVIEW BETWEEN CLASSES

Interference means that I get similar bits of information confused when they are not separated. Material that is either similar or presented very close together without time in between is not stored in separate categories, so I end up throwing it all away as disorganized "junk mail."

The answer is to schedule college courses with breaks in between for immediate review of notes *if at all possible*.

Due to when courses are offered, this may be unrealistic, but this is what to aim for. If a back-to back schedule is unavoidable (as it often is), I make a deliberate effort to distinguish between the two courses.

I use different colored paper or ink to take notes in each course, or use different notebooks. Anything I do to distinguish between the courses and their respective material will help. The most important thing is that I consciously differentiate.

KEEP COURSES DISTINCT FROM EACH OTHER

I work with my courses one at a time with at least a 5-minute break to

TAKE A BREAK AFTER EACH IDEA

get a snack, take a walk, rest my eyes, wash dishes, or do a job that doesn't require me to think. After the short break, I quickly write down the main points of what I just went over. When I give each idea its own attention, I recall not only the major points in order, but also the sub-points and even many of the details as I remember the examples that made sense of the whole lecture. Instead of being a time of mental rest, it is really a time to sort through and organize what has just entered through the door.

> *Caution: I don't want to play video games, text-message, watch TV or put in any new information from a different source during these breaks. I need the break time to organize in an uncluttered space.*

ACTION #7 = MAKE COMPARE & CONTRAST CHARTS
RESEARCH PRINCIPLES: *DISTINCTIVENESS + GENERATION EFFECT*

> *Marie likes to draw a line down the middle of a page and make a compare-and-contrast chart (see Figure 2, p. 26). As she reads the textbook, she puts it together with her notes from lecture. She likes to group the information in each column by similarities and differences. When she comes to a question she has, she circles it in pencil, to be erased when she finds the answer.*

As I think about *relationships* and the *attributes* that make each idea different, I am deeply into the heart of organization. Not only do I gain understanding of the material, but the information is burned deeply into my memory by all of the complex mental activity I am generating. I set up a permanent "file" where future details can be added. Building distinctiveness by noting the differences, similarities and relationships between information constructs cohesive pictures that I will remember long after the course is over.

Many studies have shown that the key to recalling textbook information is organizing ideas and relating them together. I remember far better when I organize by relationships while clearly separating groups

NOTICE SIMILARITIES & DIFFERENCES

of facts. Organizing *by relationship* emphasizes similarities and making ideas *specific* emphasizes differences. In other words, compare and contrast.

By noticing the differences and similarities between ideas, people, time periods, etc., I form an original concept, a single picture of the course material. One of the most powerful features of this technique is that I generate *original* categories for sorting. This produces far better recall than if someone else makes them. Researchers call this the "generation effect." Originating groups and ideas increases the processing of relationships that generates active brain waves, which multiplies memory. A domino effect.

> **GENERATE ORIGINAL CATEGORIES**

ACTION #8 = THE ART OF ASKING QUESTIONS
RESEARCH PRINCIPLE: *ELABORATIVE INTERROGATION*

Research shows that one of the most successful techniques for setting something into memory is to ask and answer questions. This is the purpose of workbooks and study guides.

There is something about asking and answering questions that brings together previous experience with a subject. Often, textbooks will insert questions after sections in the reading. But even if they don't, I form questions by asking, "What does this mean?"

There are four reasons why this is important. First, questions link new information to what I already know and understand. They help integrate course material because I draw from prior knowledge to answer them, which develops stronger interconnections among facts. Second, questions reveal what I don't know.

> **QUESTIONS LINK NEW MATERIAL TO WHAT I KNOW**

Third, questions provide a focus for attention and set memories. Fourth, they provide

> **QUESTIONS REVEAL WHAT I DON'T KNOW**

direction and momentum as they propel me forward into new "aha" experiences and the entire subject-picture falls into place for me.

With questions, information has an immediate, practical purpose (to solve a problem). I am satisfied when all questions are answered because I am *naturally geared* towards solving problems and generating correct answers develops interest in the subject. I like what I know.

ACTION #9 = DRAW & COLOR-CODE CHARTS & DIAGRAMS
RESEARCH PRINCIPLES: *DISTINCTIVENESS + IMPLICIT MEMORY*

Pictures help me remember new ideas. The saying goes, "A picture is worth a thousand words." This is logical, since

1. organization develops a picture

2. creating pictures of the material is an essential part of full mastery of course information

3. the process is dramatically accelerated when I see or produce a picture in the first place.

> **I THINK IN WORD-PICTURES & IN PICTURE-WORDS**

Because I think in word-pictures and in picture-words, I get the powerful feeling that a light has been turned on and I see things clearly for the first time when I come to understand something new. I may even say, "I get the *picture*," "It's *clear* to me," or " I *see* what you mean."

Short-term memory can be viewed as a work area where I bring pictures back to mind in order to apply them to new situations. Researchers call this "working memory." To encode actual images (pictures) helps me to chunk information for easy and efficient storage.

> **MEMORY FOR COLOR IS AUTOMATIC**

Using color makes sense because memory for color is automatic. The research term is "implicit memory." I recall shapes, colors and locations without conscious effort. This is why color-coding the charts and diagrams I draw helps clarify concepts and is so very powerful.

Alex made charts of everything. He found it especially helpful to color-code his charts and draw pictures of whatever he found confusing. When he read his texts, he looked at the pictures first to get the focus of the chapter before he ever began to read the content. Just as research found, Alex recalled the information far better on all of his exams when he related to pictures than when he only relied on his notes and written text.

ACTION #10 = STUDY FOR THE TYPE OF EXAM I WILL TAKE
RESEARCH PRINCIPLE: *ENCODING SPECIFICITY*

Knowing the *type* of questions I need to answer on an exam determines how I organize concept details efficiently. Research calls this "encoding specificity." Taking the first exam reveals the format for future tests, whether multiple choice, essay, true-false, etc. I can also ask my instructor. *Each type of question requires a different preparation for maximum efficiency.*

DIFFERENT TYPES OF EXAMS REQUIRE DIFFERENT PREPARATION

When I am going to have a multiple-choice exam, I look at the material from the viewpoint of term definitions, basic relationships, and important principles. Depending upon the course and the textbook, definitions may be the focus, or more complex understanding of names or concepts may be the exam's objective.

There are both data-based and concept-based multiple-choice exams. (Data-based questions test on glossary definitions and bare facts, while concept-based questions test on complex ideas, requiring thought integration and identification of principles.)

Whatever the emphasis, I make sure that the same emphasis is the focus of organization, and that I am able to write out course material *from that standpoint* in order to accurately communicate my mastery of the topic.

Research discovered that students get the best grades when they encode the information in the same form as the test questions. The closer the test questions

> **BEST GRADES WHEN STUDY CUES = EXAM CUES**

are to the form in which students organize the information, the better their scores. Changing the wording on exam questions sets up barriers for communication.

This also applies to all aspects of the environment in which I study,

> **ENVIRONMENT & INFORMATION STORE TOGETHER**

both internal and external (research calls this "the context effect"). As I study, *every*thing gets encoded together as a package along with the material. The closer the questions are to how I have organized the material, where I was and even the flavor of gum I chewed when I organized it, the easier it is for me to demonstrate all I know. Because the learning environment acts like a set of memory landmarks to guide me through the exam, I keep these elements as consistent as I can.

> *Nick is determined not to let the same thing happen twice. The last anthropology exam was a disaster. Although he prepared for hours, Nick nearly failed it because he had studied only definitions and details while Prof. Piltdown asked mostly essay questions. This time he was prepared.*
>
> *First, he checked with Prof. P to find out if the test format was similar to the last one. It was. Okay, now Nick knew he was studying for an essay test. So he went beyond organizing the key terms in the material and worked on understanding how they related together, writing out essays on the main concepts for practice. Even if Prof. P threw in any matching or True-False questions, he was ready.*

Instructors typically tell students what *type* of test they will be giving. Because they are aware of this memory principle, teachers at some schools even provide library access to some of their old exams as study models.

34

Habit - PACING

Getting into an effective rhythm by pacing the study process correctly saves me countless headaches and many valuable hours. It makes study almost effortless. Like a baseball player, I can have the strongest swing in the major leagues, but if my timing is off, I never hit the ball.

ACTION #11 = READ & REVIEW IMMEDIATELY AFTER CLASS
RESEARCH PRINCIPLE: DECAY

Research warns me that when I first encounter new material, it is processed shallowly and subject to what research calls "decay." It is altered by the interference of other classes and by conversations or experiences with friends that occur before I can go over the material a second time to cement it.

So, when I review material *immediately* after it is first presented, I remember it *far* better than if I wait. Because there is less in the way, it is clearer and easier to recall. I can't afford to wait. I remember parts of the class session that I had not recorded in my notes, giving me a more complete picture.

TO SEPARATE INFORMATION: REVIEW CLASS #1 + PREVIEW CLASS #2

Instead of talking to the person sitting beside me while I am waiting for the next class to start, I glance over the notes from the previous class and pick up the text for the upcoming class, quickly flipping through the pages of the chapter to be covered.

I clearly separate the information into categories so I won't have to sort through it later when it is all a jumbled mess. This contributes to both organization and my overall confidence that I have a clear picture.

> **IMMEDIATE REVIEW = EASIER RECALL**

Research shows that the brain works like breaking in a pair of shoes (every time I put them on they are easier to wear). In the area that relays memories to their storage places, there are certain cells that change permanently to allow easier recall when I go over information a second time right away.

Overall, I don't wait to review class notes. I also do required course work *as soon as possible* after class, *especially in math*. (This is one of the reasons why procrastination kills memory – please see Appendix III.)

CREATING A SUCCESSFUL AFTER-CLASS RHYTHM

1. *Follow up the lecture session with a quick review of the notes.*

2. *Rewrite the notes (better yet, type them out in an organized form to use both sides of the brain), adding other information I recall.*

3. *Read text material related to the lecture topic as soon as possible after class.*

4. *Write questions about the material. They become a study guide.*

5. *Self-test after every major sub-topic as I read.*

6. *Ask all questions before the exam. Clarifying questions greatly reduces stress and makes recall easier.*

Investing the same amount of study time at the *beginning* of a 1 - 3 week period between exams yields *at least twice* the results than if I spend it all at the end. An additional benefit is that I have plenty of time to review repeatedly before the test. I can do the same work, but have better results with proper rhythm.

> *Brianna breathed a sigh of relief and closed her notebook at the end of class. As she crowded out of the room, she couldn't wait to get to the Commons and buy some lunch, talk to her boyfriend, and relax. Later that evening, she had to work and it wasn't until the weekend that she even cracked open the textbook.*
>
> *Sunday night, as she opened the book to read the chapter for the past week, she thought, "Oh, my! This doesn't look familiar at all. How does this fit into what Prof. Thesis was saying? What <u>was</u> he saying, anyway? Looking at her notes for that day, she came to two unfinished sentences she had scribbled and some single words next to a partial outline. In the margins she had noted that an assignment was due next week and she remembered thinking, "That's so obvious. I won't forget that." So she hadn't written it down. Oh boy!*
>
> *In a panic, Brianna tried to phone the girl who sat next to her to get the assignment and to find out what those sentences could have been, but she didn't have her number. She called a mutual friend to get it. Her friend wasn't home, so she tried two others without success. Finally, she got hold of another student's number who was also in the course. Forty-five minutes later she settled down to study, hopeful that the information given her by the fourth person she called was accurate. No, that person hadn't written down those same sentences in that way and no, he wasn't sure of the assignment, either.*
>
> *Not only did Brianna waste nearly one precious hour of prime thinking time and manage to short-circuit her study plans, but she decreased her confidence and added a good dose of memory-robbing anxiety to the mix. All because she didn't go over her notes immediately, while they were fresh in her mind and she could remember easily what Prof. T had said about the course material and the assignment.*

I build a picture of the material presented in class most efficiently by: 1. reading the corresponding text material as soon as possible after class and 2. making note of how the lecture material fits.

Once I have all the information, digesting and assimilating it happens automatically, just like my stomach digests food. It is an automatic process.

Even if I only review my notes once before leaving for work or a sports event, I am working on the material while I am engaged in other activities. This is especially effective in math (Please see Chapter 5 - Mastering Math).

> **I DIGEST INFORMATION AUTOMATICALLY**

ACTION #12 = ONE SECTION AT A TIME & KEEP IT SHORT
RESEARCH PRINCIPLE: *SERIAL POSITION EFFECT*

Research shows that I remember the first and last items I read, while the middle information gets lost (the "serial position effect"). Knowing that this happens, I work with less material at a time for shorter periods so that *there is no middle* part of a long chapter that I know will be forgotten.

I cover an amount of material *small enough that I can recall the entire "chunk" easily*, like one section in my textbook that is organized around

> **I ONLY DIGEST SMALL PIECES**

a single topic. As I sort information and notice differences and similarities, the section is stored in context and recalled as a unit or concept, linked together by association, meaning and organization.

This is where my book notes and the "chapter map" come in. Because I drew out a diagram showing how the chunks relate within the big picture, I continue to fill the files with necessary data that have a place to fit.

Although there is a direct relationship between how often I repeat (rehearse) information and how fast and completely I recall it, I can review multiple times and still not recall what I need if I have not actively organized what I am repeating. Repetition without organization yields

> **REPETITION WITHOUT ORGANIZATION IS A WASTE OF TIME**

poor memory, while repetition *with* organization yields superior memory. Organization *must* precede repetition or I am wasting my time.

I schedule study time in blocks of no longer than 20 minutes, which

PROFITABLE STUDY SESSIONS = 20 MINUTES MAXIMUM

is the length of my productive attention span. I will use that time working with the organizational system, reading *only* one section of the text and writing down the main idea *in my own words*.

Then, I take a short break. A solitary, relaxation break is best. No TV or video games, conversation or text messaging that interfere with storing what I just read. I walk the dog, do the dishes, go to work or play with the kids. After at least 5 minutes, I go back and tackle the next section the same way, refreshed and ready for a new idea. During the time between sessions, I assimilate the information and organize it *automatically*.

I read a section and stop to care for children needing attention, or read one before I drive to work, or read one during coffee and lunch breaks at work. Merely grouping information together the first time I encounter it and separating study sessions by some type of break helps me tremendously later on. Long, unbroken study sessions are not a productive way to approach material.

> *Chandra was scared to take Geography 101. She heard it was a lot of reading and she knew she had to work evenings at the hospital. How could she do it?*
>
> *She tried reading one chapter section just before she left for work, reviewed section one and read section two at her first break, and a third one at her lunch break. When she got home, she reviewed and read the last section and went to bed. The next morning, she skimmed over what she had read and finished the few pages left in the chapter before class.*
>
> *Not only was she ready to understand the lecture material, but she had a clear picture of the subject. She remembered the lectures better so she needed*

less time to make sense of her notes and she could do well on the exam. She had not spent very much time at each session, but during the time she was driving and working, she was working on her geography, too!

She was in a successful rhythm.

ACTION #13 = REVIEW TEXT & LECTURE NOTES <u>DAILY</u>
RESEARCH PRINCIPLE: *SPACING EFFECT*

Why do I need to review my notes daily after I read the text? Because the task of acquiring new concepts occurs in stages, and it is extremely important to *allow time between* reviews of the same material to let information gel together. This is known as the "spacing effect."

New information is processed automatically after I first encounter it. Then, every time I review it is taken out, dusted off, *corrected for errors and re-filed* in a more correct form. Allowing time between study sessions enables

SOMETHING IN EVERY COURSE EVERY DAY

me to lay down increasingly accurate memory tracks which are strengthened by repetition and elaboration (questions and self-testing). This also prevents me from forgetting over weekends and holidays when there is no class. I do something in every course every day.

Repetition is based on brain function. When I am actively focused, my nerve cells are stimulated to grow new branching connections between each other. The pathways become both more strongly wired together and more sensitive every time I repeat organized information, requiring less effort to communicate the next time.

Every time I go over new information, I continue to inter-relate it with other items and build increasingly complex ideas as the concepts become

DAILY REVIEW BUILDS CONCEPTS

solidified in a corrected form. This prevents memories from decaying and constructs a solid foundation for further learning.

I need time to digest the information bite I have just fed the "brain-stomach" that processes information *regardless of what I do*. Then, if I take just 5-10 minutes daily to actively review my text and class notes, jotting down the differences between ideas, I re-consolidate and construct a memory pattern I cannot forget. I am making the most of my valuable time and spending less time over all.

It takes time to think. Research found that it takes time to lay down complex memories: between 2 days and 2 weeks. Here is another powerful reason for not cramming, for starting to build

IT TAKES AT LEAST 2 DAYS TO PROCESS NEW INFORMATION

images immediately after my exam on the previous material, and doing work immediately after class to allow at least 2 days between the time I first encounter a concept and when I need to retrieve it on an exam.

ACTION #14 = GET A GOOD NIGHT'S SLEEP AFTER STUDY
RESEARCH PRINCIPLE: *MEMORY CONSOLIDATION*

I can remember times when I have dreamed vividly about what I have just studied, or times when I have awakened in the morning with the answer to a thorny problem I was working on the night before. This phenomenon is so common that dreaming is viewed as a state of problem-solving.

Research has proven that REM (Rapid Eye Movement) sleep, the time when I dream vividly, is when new memories are sorted and laid down into permanent storage. It is *required* for complete and accurate retention of new concepts. Research calls this "memory consolidation."

Because of this inescapable, powerful fact, I *cannot afford to* go without sleep in an attempt to "learn" new information within a short period of time immediately before an exam (cramming, or all-nighters). It simply doesn't work. I end up overtired, frustrated,

CRAMMING *NEVER* WORKS

anxious and unsuccessful. The excess adrenaline I generate short-circuits recall of whatever memory I *do* have. (Please see Chapter 9 — The End of Test Anxiety.)

NO SLEEP = NO MEMORY

For maximum retention, I sleep following study sessions and allow at least 2 days to process new information before taking an exam. This means pacing to allow plenty of time to review and store. This is another reason why procrastination kills memory. (Please see Appendix III.)

Habit - OVERLEARNING

A common student mistake is to stop working with material once I understand it. Research has shown that the more I rehearse material I already know, the deeper I understand and the longer I remember it. This extra practice is called "overlearning."

ACTION #15 = MAKE INFORMATION PERSONAL
RESEARCH PRINCIPLES: *SELF-REFERENCE EFFECT* + *GENERATION EFFECT*

The key to long-term memory is meaning, and *personal* meaning is even more powerful. Research tells me that there is a close relationship between personal significance and recall. I remember phone numbers, dates and times that I consider important.

I don't forget what relates to me or is significant. Otherwise, I would be on continuous sensory overload as I remembered every trivial event. I am constantly cleaning house, casting off low-priority memories.

> **I REMEMBER WHAT RELATES TO ME**

To recall course material over the long term, I make it personally meaningful. However, not every course holds personal interest and few are directly related to everyday life.

One of the easiest and most powerful ways to remember the meaning in *all* courses is to write it *in my own words in an organized form.* Whenever I organize anything new, I automatically construct the categories that set up easy recall. When I write it out in my own words, I never forget it. Simple, but oh, so powerful.

ACTION #16 = SELF-TEST FREQUENTLY
RESEARCH PRINCIPLE: *TESTING EFFECT*

There is something about testing that almost seems magical. It is known as the "testing effect." Self-testing simply verifies that I am able to explain what I have learned. Also, research shows that students who test themselves show greater memory for new subject matter. In fact, the *more often* I write

> **THE MORE I TEST, THE BETTER MY MEMORY**

out complete explanations of course concepts without referring to my text or notes, the *better* my memory for them. There are three reasons why.

First, I quickly discover what I do not understand, which sends me back to course material to research and re-think what I have missed. Second, repeated testing allows me to filter out layers of wrong information as I take it out, dust it off, fix my mistakes, and re-file it in a corrected form. Third, answering questions makes information intensely personal, and anything that *I* put together is remembered longer and in a more useful form than something organized by someone else.

The most effective practice is the "blank piece of paper test." (Just like the actual exam, where the answers will be blank.) Laying out something on a blank piece of paper requires me to look at the material in a different way than just once-over reading and shallow comprehension. Reconstructing it without reference to books or notes, writing out basic concepts and essential details builds a solid picture that is ready to use on all types of exams or for doing math problems. I am also learning *how* to explain it as I will be asked to do on the exam.

> *As Ben finished one section his art history reading assignment, he practiced writing out the main ideas without referring to his text or notes. Then, he went back over his book notes to see if he had missed anything. For his psychology course, he answered the practice questions at the end of the chapter and looked up what he didn't know.*

There is no more powerful way to set memory than to self-test. The process involved in the complex recall of explaining concepts to someone else (in person or written) is the primary way to move information from short-term memory to long-term memory. Also, information gets corrected and refined every time I recall it. This consolidates memories.

SELF-TESTING CONSOLIDATES INFORMATION

Research found that when tutors in college courses were tested many months later on their subject, they remembered far more (80% vs. 20%) than the students they tutored. Step 1 = learn a subject (fully understand); Step 2 = Learn how to explain it. Explaining what I know sets deeper memory.

EXPLAINING SETS MEMORY DEEPER

So, I choose a particularly challenging concept, take a blank piece of paper, pretend it is a test question, and practice writing it out without referring to the text or notes. I identify problem areas when it is not a threat to my grade. Then, I go back to course material, correct my responses to the questions and try it again. I persist until I master all ideas in an organized form so I know I am well prepared for exam day.

> **By self-testing, I:**
> 1. **organize the course material**
> 2. **discover & identify areas of uncertainty**
> 3. **correct my errors**
> 4. **consolidate an accurate picture**
> 5. **make the information personal**

ACTION #17 = TAKE A PRACTICE EXAM
RESEARCH PRINCIPLE: *TESTING EFFECT*

I practice anything I want to be good at, so I practice taking tests.

PRACTICE THE TEST FORMAT

When I take an exam without practice, it feels like I am slogging through a field of heavy mud. Could I successfully play in a championship basketball game after only practicing on a soccer field? I need the same type of practice conditions that I expect at the exam in order to do well.

In addition to continuously self-testing as I study, I make up a practice test covering all the material that will appear on the next exam to rehearse taking it in the same format. For timed exams, I time myself.

PRACTICE TESTING FILTERS OUT WRONG INFORMATION

I am now far more prepared and assured that I know the information. This final shift from passive to active thought puts me even further into the driver's seat where I am fully responsible. I am viewing the information in a totally different way, filtering out incorrect possible responses. As I identify gaps in my understanding and seek out the answers, I increase my knowledge base and decrease test anxiety. I know the material thoroughly because I have made it my own and have taken it to the ultimate level.

> The week before her exam, Alicia made up a practice test from her algebra homework questions, using the same number of problems as the test would have in the same format as her instructor gave her before. She set her kitchen timer for 10 minutes less than she would have in class and practiced them until she could finish in time with 100% accuracy.
>
> When she took the actual exam, she was no longer afraid she could not complete the question in the time allowed, she knew the operations in logical order and aced the test. She had gained confidence in a subject she never thought she could master and conquered her math anxiety.
>
> Alicia overcame the temptation to think she could skip the practice test because of the "illusion of learning," recognizing that the problem was done correctly, but not being able to recall it without help. Recognition memory and recall memory are different.

Overall, making up a practice test produces two essential benefits: First, I identify and correct what I still am not sure of before the exam. For example, when I make up questions for multiple-choice tests, I have to determine which is the correct answer and which others are incorrect, which develops distinctiveness for the right ones. And distinctiveness = perfect recall.

MAKING UP MC QUESTIONS DEVELOPS DISTINCTIVENESS

Second, it becomes a "dress rehearsal" that trains me to demonstrate my understanding in an organized form under pressure. It removes any possible test anxiety because I know what to expect and am completely prepared with the knowledge I need to successfully demonstrate all that I know.

Practicing taking exams is a valuable learning tool. Because there is so much at stake it only makes sense that I should take exam practice seriously.

Olivia is in her second year of college, working hard to qualify for the nursing program. Juggling her part-time job with Microbiology, Human Anatomy, English Literature and College Algebra is a challenge.

Being aware of her time limitations, she refers to her master calendar to identify the day's course tasks and regularly previews the next lessons in order to be primed for classes. She begins on the next subject immediately after each exam and does homework immediately after each class, so she is free for work later on.

At home, Olivia reads only one idea at a time, makes sure to organize all class and book notes clearly by color and put concepts into her own words, including creating charts to highlight distinctions and make information personally meaningful. She self-tests daily and faithfully takes a practice test before every exam.

At the end of the year, she was tired, but elated that she was accepted into the program and made the Deans' List, despite her challenges.

ACTION #18 = CORRECT RETURNED EXAMS
RESEARCH PRINCIPLE: *MEMORY RE-CONSOLIDATION*

Learning does not stop at the exam. All forms of test, including graded exams, are an integral part of the learning process because they re-consolidate corrected information. I faithfully correct all returned work before filing it away for later review before the final exam.

This identifies and corrects what I still do not know or could not explain clearly, which prevented me from demonstrating 100% mastery of course content. One indicator that I am seeking

CORRECTED EXAMS = 100% MASTERY

WRITE OUT THE CORRECT ANSWERS

100% mastery in a course and not merely grades is that I correct all questions I miss on an exam when it is returned.

As soon as it is returned, I highlight the questions I missed and write the correct answer in a different color ink beside the incorrect one. This shows where I went wrong later on when I am preparing for the final exam in a few weeks. Writing down the correct answer both ensures that I will not forget and cements the proper answer before I move on to the next topic.

Even though exam correction is important for all subjects because it builds an accurate picture of course concepts, correcting exams is particularly important in courses that build with increasing difficulty over the term, such as philosophy and math. (Please see Chapter 5 Mastering Math)

CHAPTER 3
A 7-STEP STUDY PLAN

$\mathcal{N}$ow that I know the actions that follow core memory principles, I put them together in a study plan that works for any course. This plan has 7 steps.

STEP #1: PREVIEW MATERIAL - Establish A Context

Previewing is critical because it establishes context, constructs a framework for information to fit, begins to develop concepts and allows me to retain details the first time I read or hear them.

I previewed the course syllabus to see the topics at the beginning of the term and I preview each class session before I go. When I sit down with my textbook, I preview before I read. So, before I begin, I briefly:

STEP 1
- **FLIP THROUGH THE CHAPTER**
  - **primes mental set to absorb chapter content**
- **NOTICE THE DIVISIONS BETWEEN SUB-TOPICS**
  - **builds the big picture**
- **WRITE DOWN DIVISION TITLES**
  - **lays out the flow of ideas**
- **CONSTRUCT A CHAPTER MAP**
  - **forms a framework where data can fit**

Previewing forms a structure for everything else I do. It sets me up to listen intently in class and guides my organization as I read. The building process continues even while I am sleeping on it after organizing the information.

STEP #2: READ ONLY ONE SECTION AT A TIME - Fill In The Details

Because I only process one concept at a time, I only *work with* one at a time to keep them separated. I fill in my "chapter map" as I read:

STEP 2

- **ONE TOPIC ONLY**
  - **processes one idea at a time**
- **WRITE DOWN WHAT I WANT TO REMEMBER**
  - **filters & prioritizes**
- **WRITE DOWN GLOSSARY WORDS (words in bold print)**
  - **establishes landmarks**
- **20 MINUTES MAXIMUM**
  - **respects attention span**
- **TAKE A 5-10 MINUTE BREAK**
  - **provides time to separate concepts**

Encoding topic by topic files each piece clearly, with no interference, prioritizing what is important. Studying for small periods of time, only one idea at a time stores concepts separately. So, when I encode in little bits, not only do I remember more, but I find the mechanics of study far easier.

STEP #3: ORGANIZE THE INFORMATION - Build Understanding

Because organization is an active process, it is my entire focus in this phase of study. When course content is organized, it is clear. When it is clear, it is distinct. When it is distinct, I experience perfect recall. So, right from the first time I choose my courses for the term, the entire process of study is directed to building a completely organized, clear picture of all course concepts.

STEP 3

- **IN CLASS, LISTEN ACTIVELY & INTENTLY**
  - **- establishes concepts during class**
- **TAKE CLASS NOTES CLEARLY (best to write questions)**
  - **- records context for later refinement**
- **DEVELOP DISTINCTIONS AMONG CONCEPTS**
  - **- cements personal understanding**
- **COLOR CODE DIFFERENCES**
  - **- sets up automatic recall**

Organizing systematically and *originally* uses the entire brain in an active way. This is the exact process my instructor uses to prepare for class in order to teach the topic. Clear organization by an active mind = understanding.

STEP #4: REVIEW DAILY - Refine My Understanding

As I look over and refine my organized information every day, I have a chance to fix any errors I made the last time I saw it. Just like correcting mistakes when I type a paper, the brain-computer never saves the old errors, only the accurate version.

STEP 4

- **ADD NEWEST INFORMATION WHERE IT FITS IN**
  - **- gathers additional details**
- **REVIEW ALL INFORMATION FROM THE BEGINNING**
  - **- builds understanding within a context**
- **REFINE MY ORGANIZATION**
  - **- clarifies concepts**
- **BUILD A PICTURE**
  - **- ensures accurate understanding**

I file away concepts that are corrected.

STEP #5: SELF-TEST AS I GO - Test for Accuracy

Every day, after I complete my assignments or finish reading my text, I make sure I understand what I was working on before I put my books away. This is an ongoing process.

STEP 5

- **WRITE OUT MY ORGANIZATION**
  - **- reveals all that I know**
- **RESEARCH WHAT I DON'T KNOW CLEARLY**
  - **- discovers errors**
- **REPEAT THE PROCESS UNTIL CORRECT**
  - **- develops an accurate, complete picture**

I can't possibly retain all of the information I merely read. Self-testing ensures that the concepts are right before I sleep on them. This avoids storing wrong information.

STEP #6: PRACTICE EXAM - "Dress Rehearsal"

There are 3 reasons why the exam (showing all that I know) requires practice. First, I discover what is still not clear. Second, a practice run beforehand makes taking the test much easier because I have done it before. Third, timing myself takes the mystery out of having a time limit in class.

STEP 6

- **MAKE UP A PRACTICE EXAM**
  - **- provides the big picture of the topics**
- **SET A TIMER FOR 10 MINUTES LESS THAN CLASS**
  - **- trains testing under pressure**
- **ANSWER ALL QUESTIONS WITHOUT TEXT OR NOTES**
  - **- builds mastery of the entire topic**
- **CHECK THE CORRECT ANSWERS**
  - **- identifies any remaining gaps**
- **TAKE IT AGAIN (until perfect)**
  - **- ensures accuracy**

Final testing develops an overall confidence and readiness for exams that totally eliminates test anxiety while allowing me to accurately demonstrate everything I have learned. There is no substitute for confidence + accuracy.

STEP #7: CORRECT RETURNED EXAMS - Guarantee 100% Mastery

As soon as I get an exam back from the instructor, I look it over immediately for any errors. This is the final step for 100% mastery of a subject.

STEP 7

- **LOOK OVER THE RETURNED EXAM IMMEDIATELY**
  - determines remaining errors
- **HIGHLIGHT THE MISTAKES**
  - distinguishes the problem
- **DISCOVER THE CORRECT ANSWERS**
  - cements an accurate picture
- **WRITE THE ANSWERS IN A DIFFERENT COLOR**
  - provides landmarks for final exam preparation

Once I correct the returned exam, I file it away systematically with my other organized course papers in a special place for tests. Then, when preparing for the final exam, all corrected tests are in order, ready for the final review.

Heather was fresh out of high school. Up to her first day of college, she had never thought about studying systematically. Even though she never developed regular study habits and always crammed at the last minute before tests, she had been in the honor society her entire time in school. Full mastery was not required.

But Heather knew deep down inside that she had not really learned anything. She had viewed school as just a place to hang out with her friends and saw keeping decent grades as what allowed her to stay there.

After her first college class, as she looked at the number of pages assigned for her first exam, she felt at a loss to memorize all of the details for which she was responsible.

A light went on: something needed to change. Right then and there, Heather made a decision to take her instructor's advice and faithfully do everything suggested to develop study habits that would work. The seven steps the instructor suggested gave her specific actions that would build successful habits and lead to success.

She was amazed at the results. By the first test, Heather noticed that she was spending less study time than she ever did in high school and getting the even better grades, she felt completely confident that she had fully mastered the course concepts, she was no longer afraid of the exams and was prepared for the final. She began to enjoy learning without worrying about grades at all.

Heather experienced the attitude shift that follows from faithfully working with how the brain learns, including both mechanics of how to organize and timing of when to organize. Effective actions develop successful habits that form an attitude to learn.

CHAPTER 4
APPLICATIONS FOR DIFFERENT COURSES

There are basically three types of courses I will encounter: content courses, skill courses, and process courses. Each type of course requires slightly different mechanics, so I want to be aware of that from the beginning.

CONTENT COURSES

Content courses concentrate on learning a volume of material knowledge. These courses include history, psychology, sociology, political science, anthropology, and all other courses that focus upon *identifying, knowing,* and *understanding* facts, ideas and concepts. These are some of the most challenging for incoming freshmen because of the massive volume of material covered so rapidly. The mechanics to use for these courses include previewing, pacing, conceptual thinking, and self-testing.

1. Previewing the text before reading gives direction to understanding and decreases study time.

2. Proper pacing sets up an effective rhythm.

3. Thinking in concepts rather than in details helps me understand the similarities and differences between ideas and cements the information as a total picture.

4. Self-testing refines and reinforces concepts and details.

Tori, 18 and an entering freshman, is browsing through the campus bookstore and comes upon the microbiology text she has to buy. As she picks up the seven-pound book she begins to worry, and as she pages through the 789 pages she wonders how she will ever be able to pass this course. "I'll never remember all of this," she mutters to herself. "And if this is only one course, what am I going to do?"

To handle all of this information, Tori needs to understand the *principles* behind each chapter and fill in the *details* as she reads. She needs to put the material into her own words, draw pictures, make contrast charts, differentiate one idea from another, self-test, and be able to write out the core concepts on a blank sheet of paper without referring to text or notes. The more she clarifies the material, the deeper level of mastery she attains.

She also needs to determine the type of testing that her instructor requires, because the instructor *interprets* and *directs* the course, and every instructor puts a slightly different emphasis on the content. This provides the proper viewpoint from which to gather and organize information as she studies.

This is different from a skill course.

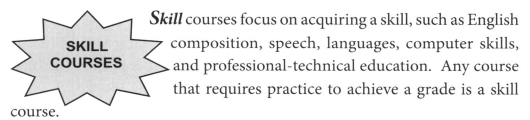

Skill courses focus on acquiring a skill, such as English composition, speech, languages, computer skills, and professional-technical education. Any course that requires practice to achieve a grade is a skill course.

For scheduling purposes, I plan on 2 hours of practice time for each in-class hour (I may need more or less depending on the task). I keep in mind the campus lab's hours or times when I can access required practice materials. I use the mechanics of listening and reading to develop a clear understanding of the procedures and engage in organized, regular practice.

1. If I do not clearly understand the information and procedures, practice will only confuse me.

2. Regular practice trains me to respond appropriately.

> *Lee found it much easier when he practiced his French assignment daily. Putting in just 10 minutes, even on weekends and holidays, kept him thinking in French and it was much easier to keep up. He spent less time overall and had a clearer picture of the sentence structure.*

These courses require hours of repetitive practice to become fluent in that particular skill. Language study focuses around a clear encoding of grammatical rules and requires vocabulary-building tasks involving visiting a language lab or making flash cards. (While glossary flash cards work well for recognition learning, such as language vocabulary, medical terminology and discipline-specific jargon, they do *not* build conceptual units. This makes them a limited technique at the college level because I cannot master concepts by memorizing definitions.)

PROCESS COURSES

Process courses involve analysis, like math, philosophy, logic or literature, where the emphasis is on the ability to reason and evaluate. They include both content and skill. Because they combine new information with new ways of thinking, they demand *consistent attention* during class to get the most from instructor feedback and interaction as I fine-tune my reasoning skills. I can never afford to miss a class.

Here, too, a good tutor can be a big help, as I have someone *listen* as I explain how I get the answers, help clarify the principles, and practice the process. Because I only remember what *I* have put together, a tutor's greatest value is to listen as I explain the process I am following and provide feedback.

Literature courses are also in this category because literary analysis involves critical thinking skills and comparison to past reading. It can only be enriched by discussion with other people, is based on abstract thought, and requires the same intense concentration during class time.

For all process courses, exams are usually essays (math problems are a form of essay because I am required to write out everything I know about

PRACTICE THE PROCESS OF LOGICAL THINKING

I FOLLOW MY INSTRUCTOR'S MODEL

a problem in a systematic way on a blank piece of paper). If I am going to communicate my competence successfully at exam time, I follow the model that my instructors use to approach the material as they guide me through the analytical process. I only get this from paying *focused attention* during class and practicing writing out the reasoning for problems explained during lecture immediately after class is over.

Also, depending upon my past experience with similar courses, I need different amounts of time to master the thinking process involved. So, I schedule time for additional practice and thought. I focus on mastering the concepts, including previewing, practice and self-testing.

1. By thinking in organized concepts rather than focusing on details, I have a picture to draw from as I explain answers to the problems presented in such courses.

2. By regularly writing out the thought processes I am learning, I am ensuring that I know them and can take an exam at any time. This is particularly critical in math.

3. Testing myself without referring to text or notes develops the patterns needed to master the material.

(Please see Chapter 5 - Mastering Math)

Patrick realized his big mistake the moment he opened up the exam package for his first U.S. history test. The questions required him to analyze similarities and differences between political parties in the first three presidential campaigns. To prepare, Patrick had made flashcards of different dates and people, but had never looked at the big picture and certainly not at any differences between political parties.

Pat had merely glanced at the example questions his instructor had put online for the class, running through the data in his head. In that moment he wished he could go back and begin all over again, following how his instructor had told the class to prepare for the exam.

Different types of courses require different preparation and no 2 are the same.

CHAPTER 5
MASTERING MATH

It is a myth that only certain people can do math. This myth floats around because math is particularly challenging to many students at the college level.

EVERYONE
CAN LEARN TO
DO MATH WELL

Within this myth is the misunderstanding that studying math is different than studying all other subjects. Or to put it another way, that some people are "mathematical," while others are "musical" or "language-oriented." However, we all encode memory for math using exactly the same principles.

Intuition is in everyone. To be intuitive is to know instinctively. Intuition for mathematics is hindered by social and cultural conditioning, such as the myth that only certain special people can understand it.

As John applied the principles of memory to the study of math, he saw his attitude begin to change. He felt it shift from feeling defeated by the impossible requirement to memorize what seemed like a ton of unrelated symbols and processes which he would never be able to understand to a feeling of eager anticipation. He was amazed that after a while he couldn't wait to see what frontiers of math he would discover next.

The miracle of comprehending the categorical definition of the problem (what is this problem saying?) was John's first major step. As he worked through the 7 steps for math success, he saw how they are based on exactly the same principles for encoding memory that are necessary for any other subject. Only the focus is different. When effective actions became his daily habits, he developed the necessary attitude to be successful in any math course. More and more he came to believe that the capacity to understand math is truly within himself.

Deciding to listen and faithfully follow every one of the 7 steps (no exceptions) in the math study plan sets mathematical intuition into motion. (Please see p. 73 - The Discipline of Unlocking Mathematical Intuition.) I am set free to see things I never thought were possible. I actually heard one student say, "math is becoming the most exciting adventure I have ever had the privilege to experience."

Let's see how the 7 steps for math success unlock mathematical intuition.

7 Steps For Math Success

STEP #1 - PREVIEW: establish a context

Comprehending the true nature of the problem is the first major step. When there are no established patterns to build on, everything that is new rolls off like water off a duck's back. So I first develop a base, a framework so information will stick.

With patterns new to me, just looking at and wondering what the

PREVIEWING IS CRITICAL

symbols mean is enough to establish a place for explanations to fit. Previewing what I am about to learn before I go to class lays the foundation for building a big picture, a context for deeper understanding. Also, I remember whatever *I* organize the *first time* I see it.

So the first thing I do is skim through the section to be covered, becoming familiar with the terms, boxes and formulas. Then I draw out a simple "map" of the section on a piece of paper (Figure 4) that establishes a framework to *fill in during class*. Without it, I soon forget the explanations provided in class because there is nothing to which they can relate. New material only sticks to existing concepts. If there is no base, I only get frustrated when I can't recall later what the instructor said because it all went "in one ear and out the other."

FIRST, ESTABLISH A FRAMEWORK

Also, if I don't preview, I end up frantically copying down the in-class problems. Because I can't keep up with the instructor I fail miserably. On the other hand, when I do preview, I come prepared and everything has a place.

PREVIEW THE NIGHT BEFORE & SLEEP ON IT

Because it takes time to process a concept, I preview the night before. During the night, the previewed information is sorted and stored, ready to be used in class the next day.

This is the easiest step to miss, but it is the most important.

I look at the section to be covered in the next class the night before for no more than 10 minutes:

1. read the objectives
2. read the headings
3. read the bold-type words
4. read the boxes
5. look over the formulas
6. write out a simple map (on only *one* page) - Figure 4

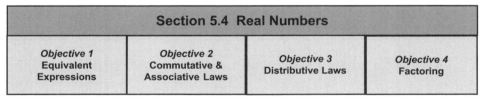

Section 5.4 Real Numbers			
Objective 1 Equivalent Expressions	Objective 2 Commutative & Associative Laws	Objective 3 Distributive Laws	Objective 4 Factoring

Figure 4

Class time is worthwhile when I come prepared.

STEP #2 - ATTENTIVE LISTENING IN CLASS: fill in the blanks

Class time provides context. During class, I listen intently to learn what the symbols mean and how to work with them in a logical sequence to solve the problems. This is in-class study. Because I only remember what I pay attention to, I follow along every step.

This means that I solve the problem along with the instructor, only jotting down my questions, the instructor's cautions (what to watch out for), and any special instructions.

ATTENTIVE LISTENING IS IN-CLASS STUDY

I focus on listening, rather than on copying. If I attempt to copy down everything written or said, I can't possibly keep up with the flow. I am in the middle of copying the first step when class moves on to the next and then the next and 4 things happen:

WHAT HAPPENS WHEN I FOCUS ON COPYING

1. I get behind in writing and the problem I was copying was erased.

2. I miss the context being provided in class because I can't listen and write at the same time.

3. I usually don't copy all of it down correctly, so I can't make any sense of it later.

4. I can't ask questions in class because I haven't identified what it is that I don't know. I go home lost and very frustrated.

However, when I reason through the problems along with the instructor, only jotting down my questions, I follow the logic of the problems in context and can match the reasoning to the symbols. I see how it all relates. Whatever I focus on, I remember.

REASON ALONG WITH THE INSTRUCTOR

As a result, I can work the problems exactly as demonstrated in class with specific questions remaining to be clarified. This maintains the connection between class and homework.

Previewing and attentive listening pave the way to recognize patterns that develop concepts which form the basis for solving future problems.

STEP #3 - DO HOMEWORK IMMEDIATELY AFTER CLASS: avoid decay

I always do the homework immediately after class, before memory of class instruction is pushed aside by information from other courses or life events. Research calls this "decay." All "unnecessary" information (anything unclear or that does not have a place to fit) is discarded. Also, interference is the enemy of clarity and clarity = perfect recall. Information not put away immediately blows away like dust in a windstorm, never to return!

> **IMMEDIATE HOMEWORK = NO DECAY**

The best possible situation for me is to have 1 hour or even 2 hours of time immediately after math class. I arrange this when I sign up for courses (Figure 5). I faithfully devote that time to completing math homework to avoid decay and have the strongest and clearest memory of the logical presentation I just heard in class. It will be stronger and clearer than if I wait until later. I remember more and enjoy my courses more because I understand what I am doing.

	Monday	Tuesday	Wednesday	Thursday	Friday
8 am	MATH 143	PHIL 103	MATH 143	PHIL 103	MATH 143
9 am	Math Homework	Philosophy Homework	Math Homework	Philosophy Homework	Math Homework
10 am	BIOL 101		BIOL 101	Break	BIOL 101
11 am	PSYC 101	BIOL 101 LAB	PSYC 101	Math Homework	PSYC 101
12 pm	LUNCH		LUNCH	LUNCH	LUNCH
1 pm	Biology & Psychology Homework	LUNCH	Biology & Psychology Homework	Psychology Homework	Biology & Psychology Homework
2 pm	WORK	Math & Biology Homework	WORK	WORK	WORK
3 pm					

Figure 5

When it is not possible for me to do homework immediately after class, due to scheduling or the necessity to go to work right away, I make sure that I take a few minutes to *read through questions* that were assigned

PREVIEW THE QUESTIONS FOR LATER

for homework and lay out space in my notebook for each assigned problem, leaving enough room to write out the steps and the reasons for them. I am primed to work the problems later on.

When I finally get to solve the problems, I am *amazed* how much I have *automatically* worked on them while I was giving attention to listening to another lecture or to tasks at work!

Homework Checklist

1. *Immediately after class if possible. This is the optimum time.*

2. *If I can't get to it immediately, at least read over the questions right after class.*

*3. **Re-work the problems my instructor did in class.**

4. *Always ask the question, "If this were a question on the test could I explain it?"*

5. *If the answer is "No," practice another, similar problem.*

*This is CRITICAL!

Only *writing out the reasons* for each step in the problems identifies the difficulties blocking mathematical intuition. The reasons verify what I intuitively knew all along. It feels like layers of fog lift with each step.

STEP #4 - WRITE OUT THE REASONS: observe patterns

Before beginning my homework assignment I repeat the example problems I saw explained in class or examples from that section of the textbook. This critical action clears up any points of misunderstanding or confusion left over from class.

As I work out the homework questions, I write out supporting reasons for each statement on paper. The easiest way (because it is

PRACTICE A STATEMENT-REASON FORMAT

organized and consistent) is to draw a line down the middle of my homework page and systematically write out each step needed to solve the problems and the reasons supporting it (Figure 6). This is called a "statement-reason format." (Please see pages 77 & 79 for further examples).

STATEMENT	REASON
1.	1.
2.	2.
3.	3.

Figure 6

Writing down reasons is the most important part of the mathematical process. Solutions are not a matter of subjective evaluation or debate. They just are.

Because solutions are standard, *I am just as able as the instructor to find them.* Because everyone is subject to the same standard, neither the instructor nor myself is the supreme authority on whether an answer is correct. We are in this quest together.

Writing the reasons verifies the solution. It is true. It is not a matter of opinion, "just how *I* do it." Because of the correct progression, it can't be any other answer. Also, if I do get a wrong answer, I can identify the specific step that does not follow logically.

REASONS VERIFY THE SOLUTION

I also see that there are reasons for everything I do. Solutions are *discovered* through understanding the problem, not generated or guessed by me. This removes all pressure to come up with something about which I know nothing. I do not guess my answers, but verify a solution that results from correct reasoning. For the first time, I relax and enjoy unraveling the puzzle in my quest to discover.

> **MY INSTRUCTOR IS THERE TO INSPIRE ME**

Because solving the problem is not a matter of guessing, but discovering what is true, it is not the instructor's fault when I can't find the solution. My instructor is there to *inspire me* to find the solution.

Providing reasons *verifies the solution* and *de-mystefies math.*

> **When I write reasons, 5 amazing things happen:**
>
> 1. I cement my memory for how to solve the problems because there is no memory without meaning and no meaning without reasons.
>
> 2. I recognize patterns that are the same between math problems, making it increasingly easier to solve others.
>
> 3. I sense that mathematical intuition is being unlocked, one layer at a time.
>
> 4. I gain confidence.
>
> 5. I develop correct reasoning.

Writing down reasons supporting each step removes many layers of confusion as the problem becomes clear. Conceptual images are held together in memory by meaning and future problems become easier.

Even though getting the right answers on homework without being able to write out logical explanations may give me homework points, I can't remember how to solve problems on the actual exam because I did not form the habit to give meaning to every step.

Some questions on the exam I can't even recognize because I never mastered the concepts behind them, resulting in a miserable failure. Even though I complained bitterly that I "knew how to get the answers" on the homework and reviews, I violated the principle, "no meaning, no memory."

REASONS ⇨
MEANING ⇨
MEMORY

Also, writing down reasons eliminates the need to memorize what to do when problems look a certain way. I no longer need to remember "tricks" of how to "get the right answer."

A famous psychologist once trained pigeons to peck at the correct answers to math problems. When they saw $2 + 3 =$ they would peck at the number 5. Their bird brains did not understand mathematical concepts. They just reacted to the symbols. Only writing out reasons ensures that I understand.

CAUTION: Solutions manuals many times show incorrect answers and few or no reasons why the steps are taken. They may show incomplete work or short-cut work steps that only leave the impression that I know how to solve the problem, but do not help me understand the reasoning involved.

To rely on the solutions manual short-circuits discovery and violates the principle, "I only remember what *I* discover with personal effort."

As a result, it does not form any lasting memory for the procedure. If I use a solutions manual for more than to *compare* my answers (being aware that *the manual may be wrong and my answer is right*) I am wasting time and money.

Finally, focus on the reasons provides meaning, lifts all obstacles to success, and eliminates my fear of math.

STEP #5 - TEST AFTER EVERY HOMEWORK SESSION: cement concepts

Homework is all about learning the concepts and checking my understanding. After I complete the homework, I write down one problem for each concept on a blank sheet of paper. Choosing ones that are difficult for me and those that may show up on the exam requires me to identify the concepts they

> **HOMEWORK IS LEARNING CONCEPTS**

represent. It sets me up to be able to do any of the problems, even the hardest ones. This establishes a mental set of responsibility and sets the brain into "active" mode, ready to remember all I do.

Then I close the textbook and work the problems. I support every step/statement with reasons before referring to the textbook or notes. In this way, I discover what I still don't know and solidify the concepts correctly.

> **DISCOVER & FIX ANY GAPS**

Then I go back, fix what was wrong and try another problem just like it without referring to the text or notes. (I easily identify where I went wrong when I write out reasons.) Testing brings about the heightened state of concentration required to set long-term memories.

When I am asleep the following night, I process only the corrected version (research calls this "memory re-consolidation"). The old, wrong answers are forgotten and replaced by accurate ones.

Completing homework accurately with 100% understanding builds confidence that I have mastered the day's work and I look forward to the next class. Also, as I preview the next textbook section, I see the big picture of the entire course and my overall mathematical mastery increases. Finally, I only remember the correct sequence of steps to answer the problems. This is the final "cap" for my homework session.

When I walk out of an exam, I know more than when I began (the "testing effect").

STEP #6 - FINAL PRACTICE TEST BEFORE THE EXAM: "dress rehearsal"

Testing is all about learning how to explain what I know. I practice everything else of importance, so why not practice taking math tests? This is so simple that I usually miss it and end up going back to thinking either

TESTING IS LEARNING TO EXPLAIN WHAT I KNOW

that math is some magical ogre that is too hard for me to learn or that only special "math geniuses" can understand it (the "math myth"). I come to feel like a "math dummy" merely because I can't write out the steps.

Just like practice is the only way around anxiety for any activity (basketball, public speaking, woodworking, you name it), the only way around math anxiety is to practice writing out the steps.

Another element of math test anxiety is that exams are usually timed. Well, I can practice that, too. No one who performs a timed activity (like Olympic track and field) just reads a book on how to run and then tries to beat the world record without timing himself every step of the way.

SET A TIMER

So, I take a practice test, the whole test, with a timer, just like the actual exam will be conducted. I make sure that I can write out all the steps in the problems on my own, without referring to text or notes.

SELF-TESTING CHECKLIST

1. I make sure that this final practice test has the same number of questions (better if it has a few more), as the actual exam.

2. I make sure that the questions represent the major concepts covered in the chapter/s. To do this, I use the list of questions generated in the self-testing part of my homework, making sure there is at least one question from every section.

3. I find a quiet place where I will be undisturbed (just like the actual exam will be).

4. I put my book aside and take the practice test just like the actual exam to discover any remaining gaps in my understanding. I wait until the very end to grade the entire test so I discover if I can move between different types of problems easily.

5. I set a timer for 10 minutes less than the time I will be allowed. This provides a cushion so I will not be rushed when I get to the actual exam.

6. I take the entire practice test without referring to my text or notes, just like the actual exam in class, writing down every step completely. No interruptions.

7. I grade my answers and correct all errors, making sure that the reasons are true.

8. I take the practice test over and over again until I achieve 100%.

The more I test myself ahead of time (with an alarm or timer signaling when time runs out), the better I can work the problems through within a limited time period. I also become used to the pressure that time brings to the activity so there is one less thing to pay attention to during the actual exam. I am less anxious because I have identified and corrected everything I wasn't sure about.

CAN I MOVE AMONG CONCEPTS?

Also, when I take the entire exam without checking the textbook, I discover whether I can *move freely among concepts* as well as among similar problems. This is one step further along than testing after every homework session. Now, concepts hold together and I develop a bigger picture of what the actual exam will be like.

Once I successfully practice taking a whole test with a timer, just like the actual exam, knowing that I can freely move between concepts and provide reasons to support each and every step for all types of questions, there is absolutely no room for anxiety. In fact, I will be eager to demonstrate all that I know!

STEP #7- CORRECT RETURNED EXAMS:

Once the instructor has returned the graded exam, I look it over to discover any errors. I highlight the notes the instructor made immediately. I go over my reasons systematically, noting where I went off track and writing the corrected step and reason in a different color for reference when I prepare for the final exam.

When I faithfully note all corrections, final exam preparation is dramatically reduced and final exams are no longer a threat. When I consider the whole picture

MASTERY IS GUARANTEED

of doing homework problems and correcting them, taking a final practice test and correcting it, taking the actual exam and correcting errors when the exam is returned, then 100% mastery is more than possible; it is *guaranteed*.

Accepting and implementing correction guarantees 100% mastery and makes 100% on any exam not only possible, but highly probable.

THE DISCIPLINE OF UNLOCKING MATHEMATICAL INTUITION
1. establish a solid foundation by previewing before class
2. listen interactively in class (follow the reasoning)
3. complete homework immediately after class
4. write out every step of every problem in a systematic form
5. self-test after every homework section
6. take an entire practice test just like the exam
7. correct returned exams

> CAUTION: Since attitude determines my success or failure, I am careful to follow the actions that form successful habits of math success. Therefore, actions shape my attitudes.
>
> I no longer say, "If I can get the right answers which will give me the grade I am looking for, who cares if I know the reasons?" I do not derail my math intuition to become once again locked in the elusive search for a grade.

Maintaining a Successful Rhythm: Weekends & Holidays

Even though I self-test every day, whenever I have a time lag between class sessions, such as weekends and holidays (Thanksgiving, Spring Break, etc.), I pay particular attention to doing *at least one math problem every day* to keep up my math habits and keep in rhythm. I concentrate on those problems I find most challenging to ensure I have mastered it all before the exam.

Although my day may be jam-packed with other responsibilities or activities, it is far more valuable to take 10 minutes and work through a math problem (self-test) than it is to spend 10 minutes on my cell phone checking social media. It is an investment in my success.

Whether it is 2 days between classes or 10 days over Spring Break, I consistently do something in math every day. I keep the rhythm going.

7-Step Problem Solving for Mathematics

Cal is enrolled in the Industrial Mechanics program at the local community college. For successful completion of the program he is required to take Technical Math 106.

For homework, his instructor assigned 10 problems. Cal began with #1.

PROBLEM 1: *Find the perimeter of rectangle ABCD. State the answer correctly to two decimal places.*

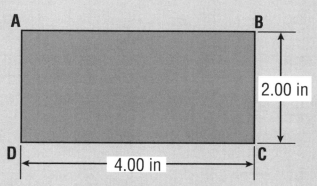

Cal is in a hurry to get his homework done because he has to be at work in an hour. So he decides to skip drawing the diagrams and previewing the problems and get right to finding the answer.

He thinks that he knows the formula for finding the perimeter of a rectangle. Without writing out the formula, he just punches the numbers into the calculator and writes down what he put in the calculator and the resulting answer.

Cal thinks that the answer is so obvious that he doesn't bother to provide any reasons to support his conclusion except that he used his calculator as he always does. He doesn't bother to check his formula or definitions.

STATEMENT	REASON
1. 4 X 2 = 8 in.	1. Calculator.

What's wrong with his answer?

Cal does all the questions the same way. The whole assignment of ten questions only took him 15 minutes. He handed in the assignment and left for work.

Next day before class starts, the instructor hands back the graded assignments. The score on his homework was 0/10 pts. with a note: "Please re-do the assignment following the 7 step problem-solving method as shown in class and hand back."

Cal is upset. Now he had two homework assignments to complete by tomorrow.

He decided that he would submit to the method that his instructor had shown in class. But because Cal thought he understood how to get the answer, he had not paid attention in class and had no idea how to work through the method his instructor had shown.

So, Cal made an appointment with the instructor and went over each of the questions in the first homework assignment.

Right after the meeting, Cal got busy. He used the 7-step problem-solving process that his instructor had laid out for the class to follow:

1. Do the homework right after class: He began working on the problems right after class.

2. Preview to understand the nature of the problem: First, Cal looked at the picture. Second, he read the directions to see what the problem was asking.

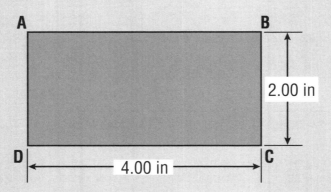

3. Determine a strategy to solve the problem: Cal had listened very carefully as his instructor had solved a very similar problem in class that day, so he knew exactly what he needed to do.

Since it was stated that the drawing was a rectangle, he looked up the definition of a rectangle and the perimeter of a rectangle in his textbook. Now he fully understood the problem and was ready to begin the process of discovering the solution.

4. Provide reasons for every statement in the work: Cal drew a line down the center of the page and began with the first statement. The drawing only showed dimensions for two sides. Based on the definitions of perimeter and rectangle, he knew he needed to find the length of the other two sides.

Applying the definition of a rectangle, Cal wrote the first statement and the supporting reason.

From the definition of perimeter, Cal knew that he had to add the length of all 4 sides. He wrote the second statement and the supporting reason.

From watching his instructor, Cal knew that the solution had to be expressed correct to the second decimal place and in the correct units. So his next statement was a statement of the solution.

STATEMENT	REASON
1. AD = BC = 2.00 in. AB = DC = 4.00 in.	1. A rectangle is a quadrilateral that has 4 right angles and the opposite sides are equal.
2. Perimeter = AB + DC + AD + BC = 4 = 4 = 2 = 2 = 12 3. Perimeter ABCD = 12.00 in.	2. Perimeter of a quadrilateral is equal to the total distance around. 3. Solution

5. Check the solution – Does the answer make sense?: Cal double-checked the question to be sure he had written the question correctly.

Next he went over the reasoning process to be sure that everything followed a correct progression.

Last, he checked his calculations to make sure that he had not made some silly mechanical mistake.

When everything checked out, Cal was sure that he had answered the question correctly. According to the definitions and principle of addition, the solution was verified and **could not be otherwise**.

6. Self-Test: *From previous experience, Cal knew that in order to be sure that he would not forget this process, he needed to do another, similar question. This time he would do it without referring to the text or notes to make sure that he really understood the concept.*

He worked similar problems until he could do them with 100% accuracy, just as though they were questions on the actual, upcoming exam.

NOTE: To solidify the concepts and guarantee that he could do these types of problems on an exam, Cal took the review questions in the text pertaining to the homework problems and as if they were the actual exam questions (NO BOOKS, NO NOTES, NO HELP).

Now Cal was confident that he really knew the concepts and could explain them on an exam.

7. Correct returned assignments & exams: *Cal highlighted his errors as soon as he got back all graded assignments and exams. He worked through the problems he had missed and corrected his answers using a different color so he could easily see his corrections.*

He made notes to himself what to watch out for on similar problems so he would be prepared for similar work and be ready for future exams.

Cal's friend Lisa was having a hard time in Elementary Algebra. It seemed to be arbitrary to her and not make any sense. She noticed that Cal had success using the 7-step plan for his tech math, so she decided to give it a try.

Lisa opened her textbook and found the first problem in her homework:
$$6 (11+8) = ?$$
This is how she wrote it down to discover and verify the solution:

STATEMENT	REASON
1. 6 (11 + 8)	1. given (the problem)
2. 6 x 11 + 6 x 8	2. distributive principle
3. 66 + 48	3. multiplication
4. 114	4. addition
114	Answer

Lo and behold! For the first time, it all made sense. It had meaning because she could see the reasons why the solution could not be other than 114. Plus, she could explain how she arrived at the solution. She was elated.

Even though her instructor did not require a statement-reason format, using it gave her a format to simply and correctly explain the problems on her homework and exam questions. When she used the 7 steps on all assignments and exams, she arrived at the solutions with very little effort. She could not believe how something so simple could make such a huge difference.

Lisa was so focused on the reasons for each step that she mastered all of her algebra and hardly noticed her straight As.

One student's experience:

Jack, 18, was diagnosed as having a learning disability and did not graduate from high school with his peers. Because he was always interested in designing and fabrication, he decided to enroll in the Machine Technology program at his local community college.

However, this meant he would have to take the rigorous level of math which involved algebra, geometry, and trigonometry, none of which he had passed. Even though Jack's basic arithmetic skills were above average, math for him meant memorizing meaningless, boring, and unrelated facts.

Jack did what he usually did in math class and that was sleep. But something was different about this math class; it actually expected him to explain his process for solving the problems.

Jack said that even though he tried to sleep, he couldn't. He would find himself jolted fully awake, drawn in by the challenge of having to explain the solutions in terms of mathematical concepts. The more problems Jack explained the more problems he would attempt and master.

Jack was never heard to even wonder what his grade was, because that was not his focus. He was only concerned that he could make sense of the problems and explain their solutions. At the end of the course, he ended up getting his first A ever in any kind of course.

But it didn't end there. Jack went on to earn As in Elementary Algebra, Intermediate Algebra, College Algebra and Analytical Trigonometry. When asked what was responsible for his transformation from someone diagnosed with a learning disability to getting straight As in college, he answered "I never worried about my grade, I just made sure I could explain every step in the solutions to the problems."

Some student comments:

Having to explain my reasons for performing the functions used in any given math problem greatly increased my ability to think critically and use a step-by-step approach to solving problems. – Kaylee

Using proofs to solve problems helped me start to understand the math. – Malcolm

It truly does work when having to explain each step in math. This deepened my understanding and curbed my tendency to take shortcuts, which never helped me learn it. – Ian

The use of the statement,reason format forced my critical thinking to take place. – Kanesha

Breaking down the learning process into steps helped me learn the math. –Zane

The format of having to reason out the answer develops a habit of thinking through a problem and following a process. – Antonio

Preparation & Assessment

CHAPTER 6
4 DIFFERENCES BETWEEN HIGH SCHOOL & COLLEGE

I have graduated from high school, but that is all I know right now. It may even have been several years since I have been in school at all. How is college different from what I experienced before? It turns out that there are 4 main differences between high school and college.

4 DIFFERENCES BETWEEN HIGH SCHOOL & COLLEGE

1. *Active vs. passive approach.* Taking an *active* approach to courses and *actively* organizing tasks in a hands-on way *always* works. Assuming that I can simply plug in passive habits of merely reading a book and be successful yields much frustration and disastrous results at the college level.

In high school I was fairly inexperienced at higher level academics, and therefore a somewhat passive thinker. I was only expected to take in basic facts and demonstrate that I understood at a surface level. I earned As for memorizing details and writing reports based on the ideas of others. However, in college, I am now expected to be on an active search for deep understanding, mastering concepts and synthesizing information. As a first-year college student, I find that my old ways of studying no longer work. Because the requirements themselves are different, they now *demand* an active approach to generate the brain waves necessary for conceptual long-term memory.

Also, an active mind-set continually builds a clear picture, looking for similarities and grouping similar information together, seeking out differences between ideas, discovering how the textbook is organized and continually self-testing. Everyone is a hands-on learner.

I remember what I <u>build</u> myself.

2. *Conceptual vs. incremental thinking.* Looking past the details to discover concepts is a skill I acquire. This shift in focus is a definite challenge.

It feels like I will miss something if I focus on the big picture. However, when I understand the broad picture of what an instructor is communicating, details fall into place and are far easier to remember. Rote memorization does not work and is not worth my valuable time and effort at the college level. Because details provide support for the concepts I discover, I automatically retain multiple details along with the big picture and carry them along with me to a test.

Details stick to concepts.

3. *Comprehension vs. facts.* In high school, most classes were geared toward facts and details. Because the goal was to gather basic data and skills, I was not required to comprehend material thoroughly. For example, I remember talking to one successful high school student about her history class. When I asked how she was tested, she showed me a list of 120 vocabulary terms that she had to memorize. They were isolated terms with no frame of reference, organization, or understanding. This was the course goal.

When I reach the college level, details and definitions are now used to *support* comprehension. If I haven't learned how to integrate and synthesize facts and details while looking for meaning in the material, I will have a hard time remembering course information.

Comprehension builds concepts.

4. *Synthesis & analysis vs. regurgitation.* For the first time, I am asked to do more than repeat information. In most college courses, students are graded on their original synthesis of material, on personal understanding and higher-level thinking as they support conclusions. There are opportunities to do original research papers, prepare presentations, and write essay exams of an analytical nature, including comparing and contrasting conceptual models.

If I remain in the mode of parroting back the text and notes, I never succeed. Anyone can read a book and regurgitate it. To handle college assignments successfully, I am actively engaged and seeking meaning. That is what "higher education" is all about.

I remember my own ideas far better than the ideas of others.

CHAPTER 7
PREPARING FOR COURSES

PREDICT COURSE ELEMENTS

So, here I am at the beginning of the term. My tuition is paid, I have bought my books and gone to my first set of classes. I have already begun to study. Since organization is an essential study habit, *any*thing I can do to organize my academic effort will set me up to put it together clearly.

Because previewing my syllabi gives me an overview of what I need to master, a good strategy is to first take out all of the syllabi I was given that day. These are the sets of rules governing every individual course that instructors make available at the first class session. After attending the first day of classes, I

SYLLABI SHOW THE BIG PICTURE

have noticed that not all courses operate according to the same rules. In each course, there are different ways to demonstrate my competence and achieve a grade. Would I ever play an important game without knowing how to win?

I take a highlighter and mark off the exact course requirements

IDENTIFY COURSE REQUIREMENTS

and how my grade is calculated. (For example, a course may be based primarily on exams, or exams may be minor and a final project may be 50% of the grade.) Course elements can be exams, quizzes, projects, class discussion & participation, attendance, workbooks, or any other requirement. I pay close attention to the percentages given to each particular element.

This shows me two things. First, it tells me how to distribute my effort. For example, if exams are the major part, or even <u>all</u> of the grade, I know that classroom information and textbook content will be the primary focus. Also, if a project or paper has a high percentage, I know to begin independent research early on in the term to produce a high-quality product.

Second, identifying specific requirements helps me develop a workable strategy.

By paying attention to these details, I avoid unnecessary disaster. For example, if I have a grade package that includes a sizeable percentage

> **ESTABLISH A WORKABLE SITUATION**

for attendance and I have a work commitment that may require me to miss class often, I either need to ask my employer about rescheduling my hours, ask my instructor if that requirement can be fulfilled in other ways, or change to a different section that has a smaller attendance component. I think ahead and establish a workable situation so I don't get overwhelmed and discouraged.

> **THE SYLLABUS IS A CONTRACT & A MAP**

This is essential because the syllabus is a written agreement between the individual teacher and myself to which I will be held accountable. As a student, I am responsible for reading and understanding it fully. Because it is both a contract and a map, I can't afford to overlook it. It will be my guide when I need to know exam dates, exactly what work remains to be done, and when assignments are due. This guides me through to the end.

Another powerful technique is to make checklists of assignments and reading to be done each week as I go. Completing scheduled checklists not only ensures all of my work gets done on time, but fulfilling my commitment to myself is very satisfying and develops character. Only positive results will follow.

PLANNING & PACING MY EFFORTS WISELY

Next, I establish a "master brain" (Figure 7) on a calendar that gives me lots of room to write. The large desk-pad calendars are a nice size and can be hung on a wall easily, but any type will work just as well. On this master, I mark down all of my class times, work times, and other commitments for the term, Next, I copy all of the deadlines listed on all of the syllabi, using a *different* color for each course, creating a code. Then I block off reasonable periods of social time, including trips and visits home. Finally, I use the color code to mark the assigned pages of reading for each course and the weekly lecture topics.

FEBRUARY

Week's Topics	Sunday	Monday	Tuesday	Wednesday	Thursday	Friday	Saturday
Ps Brain p. 104-135 Ph Plato p. 57-88 PS Congress p. 215-247 M Factoring p. 35-39	1	2 Psychology Test Drive Mark to Piano Lesson	3 Work 3-9 pm	4 Basketball Game	5 Philosophy Quiz Work 5-9 pm	6 Math Test	7
Ps Memory p. 294-337 Ph Aristotle p. 89-104 PS Judiciary p. 250-299 M Binomials p .42-48	8	9 Holiday NO CLASSES Drive Mark to Piano Lesson	10 Political Science Test Work 3-9 pm	11 Psychology Paper Due Basketball Game	12 Work 5-9 pm	13 Math Test	14 Valentine's Dinner with Chris
Ps Stress p. 379-441 Ph Socrates p. 106-122 PS Executive p. 301-338 M Quadratics p. 53-60	15 Home for Mom's Birthday	16 Psychology Test Drive Mark to Piano Lesson	17 Work 3-9 pm	18 Basketball Game	19 Work 5-9 pm	20 Math Test Joe's Party	21
Ps Learning p. 340-376 Ph Hume p. 160-189 PS Treasury p. 356-399 M Quadratics p. 61-68	22	23 Drive Mark to Piano Lesson	24 Philosophy Paper Due Work 3-9 pm	25 Basketball Game	26 Political Science Paper Due Work 5-9 pm	27 Math Test	28 Baby-sit for Rita

Figure 7

Since organization is an essential study habit, this basic step in visualization sets the tone for all of my future efforts. It is like viewing my school term from a helicopter. I now have a great advantage over trying to approach a task without first getting the big picture. It reduces stress by taking pressure off of what researchers call the brain's "task load" to keep track of everything.

This also serves to identify a rhythm for my actions, such as having tests every 2 weeks or every third Monday of the month. When I

ESTABLISH A RHYTHM

am organized and the course tasks are at regular intervals, I need to expend less effort in figuring out what to do next because it is built into my routine. I cannot underestimate the value of rhythm. Not only do habits produce attitudes, but getting into a rhythm frees up the brain for more important details.

PREVIEW THE TASKS

Now, I take a small break and gather my textbooks together at my desk alongside the master calendar. After the break, I take each one and flip through the pages I will cover in each course, referring to the calendar as I browse through the topics and look at the pictures.

I have just previewed the entire term, and *without any further work at this point,* I unconsciously, automatically form organized categories. This begins to build a picture of my courses so additional work will simply fill in the blanks and save hours of time later on.

PREVIEWING IS THE UNIVERSAL TIME SAVER

The entire picture is enhanced when I approach the text to read it thoroughly later. I tend to fall asleep over my books less and less because I am actively engaged in solving a problem ("what is this about?") and find I am interested in courses I never dreamed I could enjoy.

Why? It is a fact of life that whenever I master a problem, I feel a basic happiness at my accomplishment. I rise to a challenge and rejoice when I

THE BRAIN'S JOB IS TO ORGANIZE

am successful. I am goal-oriented and automatically driven to organize.

Research shows that the brain automatically organizes an overview the first time I encounter new material. I file all new information into categories of past experience because, biologically, I can't remember information any other way. If my very first encounter is in class, I spend the entire hour trying to figure out the topic and where the information fits. But, when I have already

> **PREVIEWING GIVES DETAILS A PLACE TO FIT**

previewed the material, I know which "ballpark I am playing in" so I can settle down to the business of sorting facts and organizing sub-categories within the major concepts as I read or listen in class.

TAKE ONE WEEK AT A TIME

Then, each Sunday evening, before the beginning of the school week, I take 10 minutes to browse through all of the material to be covered that week as I define and set my short-term goals. When I do this *consistently*,

> **SET SHORT-TERM GOALS**

I am amazed at how much easier it is to relate to the lectures and how much more of the information presented in class I remember after hearing it only once. I need far less study time to achieve the same level of understanding and my retention increases as I build an unforgettable concept of the material.

At the same time, by previewing a second time, I employ the principle that going over information more than once yields better retention. Here I am, prepared for the school week, having already gone over the material twice! Now, during our first hour of class, I fill in the blanks because I have already passed through the initial stage of "what is this all about?" I have gone directly to the stage of organizing the details within the concepts I have identified in the term overview and the weekly preview.

HOW MUCH TIME DO I NEED?

In college, student "credit hours" are calculated on a 2:1 ratio. This means that *for every hour of class time*, schedule *2 study hours* outside of class *each week*. For example, for a 3 credit-hour course I need to schedule *at least* 6 hours outside of class each week. **NOTE: process courses, like math, may require a 3:1 ratio to account for daily written homework (this means that I schedule up to 9 hours per week outside of class).** When assessing my workload for the term, I take this into consideration, so I don't shortchange my study, my family, my work, or other responsibilities. It helps to add up the total weekly commitment before ever registering for courses to make sure that the expectations are reasonable.

> **FOR *ALL* COURSES, I SCHEDULE IN**
> - *at least two* hours of study per week
> - *outside* of class
> - for *every* hour spent *in* class
> - as *soon* after class as possible

Also, to increase comprehension and reduce overall study time dramatically, I preview all of my texts ahead of time to view the topics as concepts rather than focusing on the details.

When I understand a concept, details follow automatically. It is like trying to take a huge pile of dirty clothes to the washer. Without a laundry bag, many pieces would drop along the way, just as details get lost without a concept to hold them together.

CHAPTER 8
PREPARING FOR EXAMS

𝕴 identify exactly how my instructor is going to test. Tests can have a variety of formats: essay, multiple choice, matching, true-false, short answer, or fill-ins. Superficial data questions require only recognition, concept-based require concept development, and essays require full mastery.

WHAT KIND OF EXAM?

The three levels of test question difficulty are exactly parallel to the three levels of memory depth identified in research: short-term, elaboration and permanent (Figures 8 & 9). Effectively answering questions on each level requires me to reach different depths in my study.

The deeper memory is stored, the longer I keep it. This principle is best illustrated by how I store things in a split-level home because things kept the longest are stored in the closets and not by the front door.

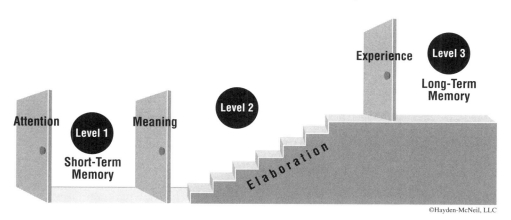

©Hayden-McNeil, LLC

Figure 8

Information first enters through the narrow door of *selective attention*, where I immediately evaluate and filter it at a superficial level so I know what to keep. Research tells me that this "entrance" (short-term memory) is an area limited to between 5 and 9 pieces of information. If another piece enters, one is pushed out like visiting friends who either leave the entrance immediately or go deeper into the house.

> **SHORT-TERM MEMORY IS LIMITED**

This means that a small amount of what I hear or read is filtered and held there briefly before something else takes its place to be evaluated. Even if I want to keep it, I can only hold so much (another reason why "cramming doesn't work.)

Whatever **means** something then passes through the second door into "long-term memory," which has many levels in itself, like climbing up the stairs. The more I organize information, the deeper it is stored.

Information passes through the third "door" of **experience** when I practicing writing it out without referring to my text or notes to work out the gaps in my understanding. This stores information at the deepest and most permanent level at "the top of the stairs." It is always my ultimate goal to reach this level. Since deep storage provides easy retrieval of any and all information, I can successfully answer any test questions regardless of format.

Recognition memory is very different from recall memory. Research

> **RECOGNITION & RECALL MEMORY ARE DIFFERENT**

shows that the two are encoded differently, the brain stores them in different places for different lengths of time, and they are used for different purposes. Recognition memory is stored at the shallowest level for the shortest amount of time, while recall memory is stored deeper and longer.

Figure 8 shows how the three levels of memory relate to the levels of depth each type of testing requires. How deep, and therefore how permanent, my memory is for course material depends upon *HOW* I encode and work with the information that comes in through my selective attention to establish and refine meaning.

If I only read the material and am just able to *recognize* the ideas or terms, the best I can do well on are data-based multiple-choice questions that ask about terminology. I am very limited. This is because I am only encoding at a superficial level, with answers

READING IS SUPERFICIAL

retrieved by superficial cues, such as what a word looks like. I won't reach mastery by just understanding definitions.

I cannot write an essay or even score well on matching or multiple-choice questions that are based on conceptual understanding. Also, memory stored at this superficial level is easily erased by the stress reaction of test anxiety.

SUMMARY OF MEMORY LEVELS & TESTING REQUIREMENTS

	ENCODING	STORAGE	RETRIEVAL
LEVEL I:	Read Text & Notes	Superficial	Recognition
Entry: Selective Attention Maximum Testing Level: Recognition (Key-Word Multiple-Choice)			
LEVEL II:	Understanding + Elaboration	Comprehension	Concepts
Entry: Meaning Maximum Testing Level: Comprehension (Concept-Based Multiple-Choice, Matching, True-False, Short Answer)			
LEVEL III:	Personal Organization	Practical	Explanation
Entry: Experience Maximum Testing Level: Application (Essay & Math Problems)			

Figure 9

Because research shows that meaning is the only way to enter the second level, all of the ways I organize by meaning (like the chapter map, chunking, and comparison charts) elaborate on the material, enrich my

MEANING = MEMORY

knowledge and store it more permanently. *Without* meaning, it remains superficial. (Even professional memory experts who memorize long lists of numbers or words assign some sort of meaning or relationship in order to recall them.)

Whenever I understand and have elaborated on the information, tying it to other concepts, comparing, contrasting and noting distinctions between ideas, I am able to tackle concept-based multiple choice, true-false, matching, fill-ins, and other types of advanced test questions. The only type of question for which I am not yet fully prepared is an essay or a math problem.

WRITTEN ANSWERS REQUIRE MAXIMUM DEPTH

To arrive at the depth necessary for a superior quality written (essay or math) answer, I practice writing out the concepts on paper without text or notes. Through this, the concepts become part of me and are now stored at the third level. I only reach this deep understanding through focused self-testing.

Course information becomes richer as I interact with it to understand, organize and put it into a form I can communicate.

Strategies for Different Tests

I distinguish between precise preparation strategies used for different types of tests so that I clearly communicate all that I know.

Because I store concepts separately, test cues direct me to the proper file to open and answering exam questions demonstrates that I have information filed away in the correct category in a complete form.

MULTIPLE CHOICE & MATCHING: Suppose I have a multiple choice and/or matching (MC/M) test to prepare for.   First, I identify the type of MC/M questions from experience with previous exams. Questions can either be data-based, concept-based, or mixed.

Here is where previewing and all of the work I did organizing the course material pays off. Because I have a thorough mastery of the concepts covered in the chapters to be tested, I am able to answer concept and matching questions.

Data questions are trickier because I have no idea which specifics will

> **DATA STICKS TO CONCEPTS**

be asked. Because data sticks to concepts, when I focus upon the concepts covered by the exam, seek out details that support them, and practice writing them out, I will able to recall them within their proper context on the exam.

TRUE-FALSE: True-false questions are testing for general understanding of the core principles that identify a concept as distinct from all others. Like multiple choice questions, they are also concept-based. Because I always target mastery of all concepts, I am able to recognize which statements are true and which are false.

SHORT-ANSWER & FILL-INS: Any form of fill-in questions requires me to recall and write down what I have learned about primary concepts. The difference is that I have to actively generate the answers instead of having them listed for me, so they involve recall memory.

While recognition memory is shallow and merely reacts to what something looks or sounds like, recall memory requires me to completely re-produce an entire concept from scratch. Writing in a short answer or filling in a blank requires me to actively understand the concept being tested, not just passively recognize.

Because I have fully mastered the concepts, I am able to explain the material without any cues, *using the appropriate terminology*. The relationship

SELF-TESTING REMOVES OBSTACLES

between the concept and the supporting data is my target and I succeed because I practiced writing out both the concept and the supporting data together as a unit. Because I have self-tested like this, I already produced the answers from my genuine understanding at least once before. Self-testing removes any remaining obstacles to success on the exam.

ESSAY: Often, acing an *essay* test seems to be an elusive mystery.

First of all, essays are written in class and I am expected to:
1. clearly address *all parts* of the question, and
2. be organized.

Here's an important principle: *anything* I can do that will help the instructor read and follow along with my answer results in a higher score. Simple, clear communication. Extensive research has shown that student written work is penalized for *anything* that interferes with the communication process between student and teacher.

Communication Barriers include:
1. **spelling errors**
2. **grammatical mistakes**
3. **small writing**
4. **poor penmanship**
5. **not enough space between lines for instructor comments**

So, I am *clear*. And in order to be clear, I am *organized* and *neat*. Even as when encoding information, distinctiveness is the key to writing out a good essay (and math) exam. Clarity is essential for both input (study) and output (preparing written test answers, even math problems), because I am required to show all steps of my work so my instructor can evaluate the process I went through to find the answer.

Here is a step-by-step way to prepare for an essay test:

ESSAY TEST PREPARATION CHECKLIST

1. Choose about 5 possible topics the instructor might test on. I identify the central themes by the topics covered in lectures.

2. Prepare a brief, 3-point outline for each topic, with 3-5 sub-points each.

3. Search out details, such as names, dates, etc., to support each statement. Add these to the outline.

4. Organize the entire picture into a complete, pre-fabricated answer.

5. On a blank piece of paper, practice writing the outlines and the details without referring to text or notes.

After this, I am able to answer *any* question on that topic, because I already researched the data I need and *stored it in a meaningful context.* I mastered the entire body of material as I thought out my test-prep outlines. I practiced organizing the information and have facts ready to support my conclusions. Because I practiced writing down the information without the aid of course materials at least once, I really do know the topic *inside and out.*

Then, when I write my essay in class, I am very careful to:

1. **Answer every part of the question clearly and systematically.** My instructor has a scoring scale (called a "rubric") of what question parts are worth how many points. For example, each part of the following 100-point essay question is worth 25 points:

> **Philosophy 101: "Compare and contrast the writings of Plato with those of Aristotle on the source of human knowledge."**
> **This question has 4 parts:**
>
> 1. **compare = similarities**   3. **Plato's philosophy**
> 2. **contrast = differences**   4. **Aristotle's philosophy**

If I don't answer one part of the question, I lose the opportunity to add those points. It is easy to begin explaining the differences and miss discussing the similarities (the question says, "compare _AND_ contrast"). This automatically reduces my possible score by 25 points, taking an otherwise correct essay answer from 100% (A) down to 75% (C).

I make sure the essay is easy to read by using clear, simple language in an organized form. I write clearly in dark print. If allowed, I use pencil so I can erase neatly and make corrections as I write. If I can only use pen, I think through my writing carefully before putting down the words to keep my paper neat.

2.   Support each point with facts & examples. Support for each point demonstrates both a clear knowledge of the details and a thorough, accurate understanding.

3.   Be _original_ in my analysis. Being original demonstrates that I can evaluate the material and have thoroughly mastered it.

When I hit these three targets in my essay answer, I get credit for everything I know because I demonstrate my mastery of the essential information in an organized and concise manner. The grades are sure to follow.

> ## *Formula for Writing a Structured Essay Exam*
>
> **Step #1** - Write a topic sentence that includes the <u>number</u> of points to be covered in each question element. For example, "There are *2* similarities and *4* differences between the ideas of Plato and Aristotle on the source of human knowledge."
>
> **Step #2** - Devote one paragraph to each individual point. Begin the first paragraph with, "The *first* similarity...." and add all of the supporting data. Then begin the following paragraphs with, "the *second* similarity.... The *first* difference...." etc. until all of the points are covered.
>
> **Step #3** - Summarize with a concluding paragraph.

Using numbers provides a structure for my answer (ex. "...*2* similarities and *4* differences..."). This clarifies communication with my instructor and allows me to demonstrate my *original* mastery of the concepts.

Beginning each paragraph with one of the numbers in my topic sentence communicates my original analysis. It is also easy to grade because the answer is stated in the same wording as the original question.

NOTE: I find it helpful to write out the essay outline before beginning to write actual paragraphs. Because it assists both writing and grading, it facilitates communication.

CHAPTER 9
THE IMPORTANCE OF DETAILS

No discussion of academic success is complete without pointing out 4 important types of details:

1. Details in course requirements.
2. Details in assignment requirements.
3. Details in note taking.
4. Details in written presentation.

First of all, I *never assume anything.* This kills my grade faster than any other single mistake. Every math class does not have the same homework system or exam format and every history teacher does not use the same grading scale. All assignments are not graded according to the same standards and missing class always means I missed something important. Submitting written material without correcting all grammatical errors or not following the required presentation style for a term paper will not earn proper credit just because the ideas are well formed.

1.   Details in course requirements.

I read the course syllabus and use it regularly to chart my progress. This document is a legal contract that lists the grading requirements, course expectations, and other critical information. In other words, it explains the "rules of the game."

I may struggle with courses simply because I haven't paid attention to specific requirements. I make it part of my weekly routine to read each syllabus, checking the upcoming tests and assignments.

THE SYLLABUS TELLS ME THE RULES

What happens when I am absent? The syllabus addresses attendance, making up missed work, or if attendance even counts towards the grade.

Teachers and classes differ.

When are assignments due? Following the schedule keeps me up to date; there may be projects for different courses due at the same time. Working ahead produces far better products that demonstrate mastery of the course.

TEACHERS & CLASSES DIFFER

How are grades determined? Are they based only on exams? How much does a paper count? What about class participation? Are there other grade components? Are tests regularly given on the same day of the week? Monday, Friday, or otherwise? Because everything affecting my prioritization and rhythm is found in the course syllabi, they are the most important papers in my notebook and I give them top priority.

2.   Details in assignment requirements.

Every assignment has a purpose. Each one develops a distinct part of the educational package, molding a more complete product. Since they are all as different as the courses I take, I never assume that what is required for one assignment is required for all of the others.

EACH ASSIGNMENT HAS A DIFFERENT PURPOSE

For example, if I am to write a paper for sociology and the assignment says "APA Style," I *must* use APA style, not MLA or any other format. If I don't use the proper form, I will lose grade points unnecessarily for not following instructions.

Why is this so important? First, because *the required format is part of the assignment*, following it means that I did all of the assigned work. It is essential to pay close attention to any formatting handouts provided. Second, I only receive full credit when my paper format matches the instructor's grading key. In math, this is "show your work."

FORMAT IS PART OF THE ASSIGNMENT

I routinely make sure I clearly understand the purpose, format, and grading standards for each assignment. If I still have questions after reading over the assignment instructions, I ask my instructor for clarification.

3. Details in note taking.

Note taking in an organized form is critical because this is how I find out what is important about the material. Lectures give structure to a course and provide a context for details. As a guide through unfamiliar territory, the instructor helps me encode course information with essential categories already identified.

LECTURES GIVE STRUCTURE & CONTEXT

However, taking notes in class never replaces listening attentively to the instructor. One cannot do both at once. The human brain can only pay focused attention to one thing at a time, including whether to listen or to write. (If I find I can't make sense of my notes at home, that is a good indication I focused on writing instead of listening to comprehend.)

Different instructors use different systems. Some require prior textbook reading and book notes so students are prepared to listen. Some provide lecture notes ahead of class or post them online, others record lectures and some do not. If lectures move too fast for me to keep up, I prepare a structured outline from the textbook to take with me.

DIFFERENT INSTRUCTORS USE DIFFERENT SYSTEMS

Regardless of the system, I make sure that complete notes include major topics, significant details, what to watch out for and questions. There may be logistical information like syllabus updates, study sheets, handouts, and class cancellation dates announced in class.

If I miss a class, *I get the notes.* At the beginning of the term, it is a good practice to swap phone numbers with at least two people to use as backup for class activity. That way, I save valuable time searching for how to contact them.

4.   Details in written presentation.

This is a critical element. Research shows how misspelling as few as 5.9% of the words in a written assignment affects not only the grade, but also how the instructor perceives a student's non-academic character. Even though teachers were instructed to consider *only* argumentation and thought quality, students were graded down an average of half a grade (some as much as 2 grades down) simply due to writing mechanics. Students' personal characters were also evaluated lower on 10 different dimensions (including honesty and punctuality) simply because

> **CLEAR COMMUNICATION = FULL CREDIT FOR WHAT I KNOW**

of a few spelling errors *that interfered with the ideas being communicated.*

Just like a finish carpenter's work quality enhances or devalues a well-built home, so writing mechanics either makes or breaks a well-thought-out written project. The quality of written work is greatly enhanced by paying precise detail to spelling, grammar, punctuation, margins, spacing, writing style (MLA or APA), paper quality, print darkness and even font type to present written work worthy of top grades.

Readability is just as critical for math. I show all work in a *readable and orderly form* to receive all the points I deserve.

I cannot go into an important job interview with a glob of mustard on my shirt and leave the impression that I am a neat and careful person, even though it may be the result of a last-minute lunch accident. First impressions count and excuses are not acceptable. When the only demonstration of my hard work is a single written product, it must meet the standard as perfectly as possible to receive proper credit.

> **WRITTEN WORK REPRESENTS COMPETENCE**

There is an important rule of thumb: *any*thing that interferes with communication between student and instructor tends to lower a grade significantly because it is distracting and makes it harder to grade. One study showed that even excessively *advanced* vocabulary decreased, rather than increased, grades. (Not writing clearly hinders communication because having to stop and figure out what I am saying disrupts the flow of a clear explanation.) This principle also applies to tiny or unclear handwriting, poor grammar or punctuation, not following style instructions, or even a coffee stain on the paper.

> **BE CLEAR**
> *******
> **BE CORRECT**
> *******
> **FOLLOW INSTRUCTIONS**

Here is a checklist that outlines the standard technical requirements for college level work. For each assignment, I check to make sure the grading targets for each assignment fit this list so that my bases are covered.

REQUIREMENTS FOR COLLEGE QUALITY WORK

1. **Word processed or typed.**

2. **Double spaced throughout. (This allows instructors to write comments between the text lines.)**

3. **Type is dark enough to read easily.**

4. **#12 or #14 font (some font styles have a very small #12).**

5. **Plain, book-style font, NO SCRIPT.**

6. **1" margins on all 4 sides of the paper.**

7. **Margins: ALIGN LEFT.**

8. **Indented first line in a paragraph (1 tab from the left).**

9. **Correct spelling (use a computer spelling check AND have it proofed by at least one other person).**

10. **Correct grammar (proofed by at least one other person).**

11. Correct punctuation (proofed by at least one other person).

12. Note: Research papers may require either APA* or MLA** format for the title page, footnotes (or in-text citations), reference page, quotations and other details. These are *very* different. Check with the instructor to make sure which style is expected and identify the *specific* requirements for the assignment.

* American Psychological Association

** Modern Language Association

CHAPTER 10
THE END OF TEST ANXIETY

$\mathcal{W}$hy is preventing test anxiety so important and how does creating effective study habits end it?

Every situation produces its own stress. Depending upon how I

TEST ANXIETY SHORT-CIRCUITS MEMORY RETRIEVAL

prepare, an exam becomes either motivation that primes me for top performance or test anxiety that short-circuits the memory retrieval system and makes complete recall of academic information impossible.

The body chemistry involved in anxiety is a #1 memory killer. The marvelous fight-or-flight stress response is built to save me from danger (exams become threats when I am not prepared). When it is triggered, I am primed to fight or run away, not to sit and think. (Remembering facts and ideas is not the most necessary element in raw survival.) While excess adrenaline in my system helps <u>set</u> memories (I will never forget where I saw the rattlesnake), it is deadly to memory <u>retrieval</u> (I don't think about physics while I am running away from it).

This means that the intense, brain-freezing anxiety that I feel at exam time is the result of not being 100% prepared. Anxiety at test time is definitely something I do not need.

TEST ANXIETY IS A BIOLOGICAL REACTION

Research shows that the *four factors* involved in whether or not the stress of an exam becomes test anxiety are attitude, prediction, taking responsibility (control) and social support. By engaging in effective study actions, I prevent test anxiety.

✔ DEVELOP AN ATTITUDE OF COMPLETE SUCCESS

I faithfully engage in effective study actions to form habits that produce an attitude of complete success. I am prepared for the exam. I understand everything completely. When I take control of course work, don't procrastinate and follow the principles of memory, I generate the active brain waves needed for learning.

> **VIEW EXAMS AS CHALLENGES**

When I view exams as challenges, rather than threats, I am free to work. Once I have succeeded, the overwhelming sense of accomplishment encourages me to tackle even more challenging courses because I have a method in place to reach my course goals.

✔ PREDICT EXAM PACING & CONTENT

Unpredicted tests increase stress. I prevent exams from producing test anxiety by predicting when they will be given, what they will cover and how long they will be.

> **PREDICTION REDUCES "TASK LOAD"**

I know what is coming in my courses by studying the syllabi and logging all of the due dates and time available for study onto a master calendar. Writing down all of the reading, assignments and exams reduces "task load," what I have to remember.

Because the brain is like a computer, its working area functions slower when it has too many "bits" of information to process at once (like keeping track of life's many details). The master calendar functions as an external "brain" to alert me to the tasks ahead.

Predicting what is coming removes the greatest source of test anxiety. Imagine not knowing when an exam is going to be given!

✔ TAKE RESPONSIBILITY

By taking responsibility, I do not let exams become crippling anxiety. I control my actions. Because I faithfully choose to engage in successful study actions, I relax and enjoy my courses. I never worry about grades because they are the natural result of complete mastery.

I control my time. Using the master calendar really helps. Every day when I walk by my desk, I see what is coming in the weeks ahead and break down course expectations into smaller tasks that lead to success. At exam time, I am ready.

> **I CONTROL MY ACTIONS & MY TIME**

The simple fact of knowing lays out the regular rhythm of my activities. When I have an event to attend, I get assignments done *before* I leave, so I'm not stressed when I get back. I pace study time for exams to allow at least the minimum 2 days necessary to process new material. With predictability and taking responsibility, my exams are manageable, although they are still challenging.

✔ ESTABLISH SOCIAL SUPPORTS

Education is a social process because it involves transfer of ideas and reasoning skills from one person to another. It is built on relationships and respect.

> **EDUCATION IS BUILT ON RESPECT**

Communication with the instructor is the core of the course. I listen attentively during class, get all questions answered, and discuss concepts with a tutor who listens to me explain course material. Their feedback is invaluable.

Making use of available social support throughout the course assures me that I have mastered the course material by exam day. There is no room for test anxiety.

SUMMARY & CONCLUSION

Summary

Memory research shows me how to study in college. To review, I have seen that attitude is the bedrock for all learning. Shifting my perspective from grades to full mastery of all course concepts totally transforms my view of school and eliminates all fear.

I have seen that proper attitudes are formed as I develop regular habits by engaging in study actions that follow principles of how the brain learns. These actions always produce success.

The 3 habits these actions produce are:

1. Efficient organization
    - ✔ I am actively focused
    - ✔ I preview before class & before reading
    - ✔ I organize the first time
    - ✔ I chunk similar information together
    - ✔ I identify similarities and differences
    - ✔ I make the concepts distinct from each other
    - ✔ I make charts
    - ✔ I ask questions
    - ✔ I use color
    - ✔ I prepare for specific types of exams
2. Proper rhythm
    - ✔ I organize immediately when information is presented
    - ✔ I only work with 1 concept at a time & keep it short
    - ✔ I review frequently
    - ✔ I sleep on what I have organized
    - ✔ I allow at least 2 days to process new concepts

3. Overlearning
  - ✔ I generate personal meaning
  - ✔ I test after every homework session
  - ✔ I take a final practice test
  - ✔ I correct returned exams

I have seen how the goal is full mastery of all course material, that I take active control of the process, that I attend to information carefully, time focused efforts properly, organize and elaborate material into concepts, and repeatedly self-test to set it into long-term retention.

These orderly principles work. There are many successful techniques that are based on them. *Any*thing I do that follows the principles will result in success and *any*thing I do that does *not* follow them explains why I fail. I can't argue with the brain's biology any more than I can expect the family car to go from a dead stop to 90 mph in 3 seconds.

The 6 biggest mistakes I made in the past were:

> 1. **Thinking that reading = study (passive brain)**
> 2. **Waiting too long to start**
> 3. **Not looking ahead before I read (not previewing)**
> 4. **Not organizing information clearly**
> 5. **Sessions longer than 20 min.**
> 6. **Not testing myself**

Conclusion

The greatest value in my education is how it develops personal character. A wise man once said that the word "education" refers to developing the complete person, including moral character, while the word "instruction" refers to intellectual activity. This means, that while instruction can be measured, education is not subject to grades.

Using nature's rules of how to remember develops an attitude of respect for others and for myself. I learn to listen, to follow instructions. I come to realize first of all, that I must follow the way the brain works or nothing happens. I see that I am subject to specific rules and cannot just do things any way I want to. Following nature's laws shapes me into a more peaceful, happy, confident person.

Thank you for taking this little journey with us through the workings of the human memory system and how they can be applied to a most important task. It is our sincere wish that all of your hard courses may become easy ones, that you may experience unprecedented success, and that you find education to be an exciting and abundantly rewarding enterprise as you discover the joy of full mastery in all subjects you undertake. May you daily see the windows of heaven (your mind) open and experience the incredible joy of learning as you use good Study Sense.

Appendices

APPENDIX I
4 MODELS OF MEMORY

Memory is a category system. There are 4 models that will help me relate to how the brain sets memory and understand its requirements:

1. The Computer

As working equipment, the brain is like a computer, a highly efficient, electronic bank of unlimited capacity. Like a computer, I program it (encoding), hold the information (storage) and output when I need to use it (retrieval) (Figure 10).

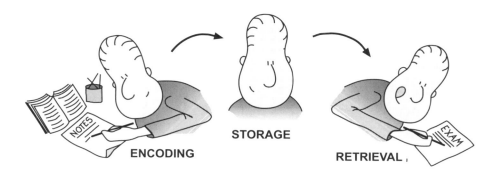

STORAGE

ENCODING

RETRIEVAL

Figure 10

With these three stages, it is *how*, not *how much time* I spend programming new material. It is my job as a programmer to encode all new information in such a way that it *can* be retrieved, in a *form* that allows me to use it whenever I need it. It would be a waste of time to encode information in a form that I couldn't access later.

2. The Filing Cabinet

The memory system categorizes information like a filing cabinet. Concepts hold data. Organizing information the *very first time I see it* keeps my mind clear. There are no unsorted piles of "junk mail" for the brain to throw away and no unclear "mud" allowed. It keeps things clean. Anything that has no file is discarded because it has nowhere to fit.

3. The Stomach

Memory processes information like a stomach: it takes time to digest new material. Memory depends both upon nerve cells growing new connections between them when they are stimulated and upon the permanent changes that occur when they are stimulated repeatedly the same way with time in between sessions for *brain-digestion to take place*. If I don't allow enough time to digest information, I can't absorb it for later use.

4. The House

Just like a house, the deeper information is stored, the longer I keep it. Storing concepts deeply ensures that I will remember it permanently.

I am constantly programming my brain-computer in usable ways, filing new information into categories, digesting what has entered, and storing it in the appropriate places.

APPENDIX II
MEMORY LEVELS,
ENTRY KEYS & TESTING REQUIREMENTS

	ENCODING	STORAGE	RETRIEVAL
LEVEL I:	Read Text & Notes	Superficial	Recognition
<td colspan="3">Entry: Selective Attention Maximum Testing Level: Recognition (Key-Word Multiple-Choice)</td>			
LEVEL II:	Understanding + Elaboration	Comprehension	Concepts
<td colspan="3">Entry: Meaning Maximum Testing Level: Comprehension (Concept-Based Multiple-Choice, Matching, True-False, Short Answer)</td>			
LEVEL III:	Personal Organization	Practical	Explanation
<td colspan="3">Entry: Experience Maximum Testing Level: Application (Essay & Math Problems)</td>			

APPENDIX III
REASONS WHY PROCRASTINATION *KILLS* MEMORY

1. Lack of preparation produces anxiety.

      +

   Anxiety short-circuits memory.

   > Lack of preparation = helplessness
   > Helplessness = anxiety
   > Anxiety = short-circuited memory

2. Memories are set by going over new information a second time <u>immediately</u>, before it fades.

3. It takes <u>at least 2 days</u> for the brain to process new information completely.

4. Memories are processed into long-term storage during REM (dream) sleep. No sleep because of cramming and / or "all nighters" totally defeats the purpose.

APPENDIX IV
18 EFFECTIVE STUDY ACTIONS

ORGANIZATION

ACTION #1 ACTIVELY FOCUS MY ATTENTION

ACTION #2 PREVIEW

ACTION #3 ALWAYS READ WITH PENCIL & PAPER

ACTION #4 GROUP BOOK & LECTURE NOTES BY TOPIC

ACTION #5 IDENTIFY DIFFERENCES AMONG CONCEPTS

ACTION #6 ESTABLISH A CLEAR BREAK BETWEEN ANY 2 SUBJECTS

ACTION #7 MAKE COMPARE & CONTRAST CHARTS

ACTION #8 THE ART OF ASKING QUESTIONS

ACTION #9 DRAW & COLOR CODE CHARTS & DIAGRAMS

ACTION #10 STUDY FOR THE TYPE OF EXAM I WILL TAKE

PACING

ACTION #11 READ & REVIEW IMMEDIATELY AFTER CLASS

ACTION #12 ONE SECTION AT A TIME & KEEP IT SHORT

ACTION #13 REVIEW TEXT & LECTURE NOTES DAILY

ACTION #14 GET A GOOD NIGHT'S SLEEP AFTER STUDY

OVERLEARNING

ACTION #15 MAKE INFORMATION PERSONAL

ACTION #16 SELF-TEST FREQUENTLY

ACTION #17 TAKE A PRACTICE EXAM

ACTION #18 CORRECT RETURNED EXAMS

APPENDIX V
REQUIREMENTS FOR COLLEGE-QUALITY WORK

1. Word processed.

2. Double spaced throughout. (This allows instructors to write comments between the text lines.)

3. Type is dark enough to read easily.

4. #12 to #14 font (some font styles have a very small #12).

5. Plain, book-style font, NO SCRIPT.

6. 1" to 1.5" margins on all 4 sides of the paper.

7. Margins: ALIGN LEFT.

8. Indented first line in a paragraph (1 tab from the left).

9. Correct spelling (use a computer spelling check AND have it proofed by at least one other person).

10. Correct grammar (proofed by at least one other person).

11. Correct punctuation (proofed by at least one other person).

12. Note: Research papers may require either APA* or MLA** format for the title page, footnotes (or in-text citations), reference page, quotations and other details. These are very different. Check with the instructor to verify which style is expected and identify the specific requirements for each assignment.

* American Psychological Association
** Modern Language Association

APPENDIX VI
A 7-STEP STUDY PLAN

1. PREVIEW THE TEXTBOOK
- ⇨ flip through the chapter
- ⇨ notice the divisions between sub-topics
- ⇨ write down division titles
- ⇨ construct a chapter map

2. READ ONLY ONE SECTION AT A TIME
- ⇨ one topic only
- ⇨ write down what I want to remember
- ⇨ write down glossary words (bold print)
- ⇨ 20 minutes maximum
- ⇨ take a 5-10 minute break

3. ORGANIZE THE INFORMATION
- ⇨ in class, listen actively & intently
- ⇨ take class notes clearly (best to write questions)
- ⇨ develop distinctions among concepts
- ⇨ color-code differences

4. REVIEW MY NOTES EVERY DAY
- ⇨ add newest information where it fits in
- ⇨ review all information from the beginning
- ⇨ refine my organization
- ⇨ build a picture

5. SELF-TEST AS I GO
- ⇨ write out my organization
- ⇨ research what I don't know clearly
- ⇨ repeat the process until correct

6. PRACTICE EXAM
- ⇨ make up a practice exam
- ⇨ set a timer for 10 minutes less than class
- ⇨ answer all questions without text or notes
- ⇨ check the correct answers
- ⇨ take it again (until perfect)

7. CORRECT RETURNED EXAMS

⇨ look over the returned exam immediately

⇨ highlight the mistakes

⇨ discover the correct answers

⇨ write the answers in a different color

Acknowledgements

Our deepest gratitude to Robert A. Boody and his dear wife, Sarah V. Boody, who inspire us to enjoy the miracle of unwrapping and removing multiple layers of confusion in order that this little intuitive message of hope could be simply and clearly communicated. Thank you for your labor, counsel and direct contributions to its heart.

We are also grateful for the help of many people over the years who have provided invaluable suggestions and encouragement: Mikal Ewing, James B. Klassen, Michelle R. Young, Peter B. Young, Luke A. Young, and Lincoln T. Young.

A special thank you to Stephanie Kern.

Also, we are grateful for the input from countless students who have each contributed in small ways over the past 16 years with their comments and continued encouragement as they applied these principles in our courses. Some would share how the book had helped them. Others would suggest what they would like to see included in this edition.

"This new attitude and its efficient mechanics not only go hand-in-hand towards success, they are success in themselves."

– Dr. R.A. Boody

References

Ader, R., & Cohen, N. (1993). Psychoneuroimmunology: Conditioning and stress. Annual Review of Psychology, *44*, 53-85.

Ader, R., Cohen, N., & Feltern, D. (1995). Psychoneuroimmunology: Interactions between the nervous system and the immune system. *The Lancet. London, 345*(8942), 99-103.

Anderson, R. C., & Pichert, J. W. (1978). Recall of previously unrecallable information following a shift in perspective. *Journal of Verbal Learning and Verbal Behavior, 17* (1), 1-12.

Ashcraft, M. H., Kellas, G., & Needham, S. (1975). Rehearsal and retrieval processes in free recall of categorized lists. *Memory and Cognition, 3*(5), 506-512.

Atkinson, R. L., Atkinson, R., C., Smith, E. E., & Bem, D. J. (1993). *Introduction to psychology 11e.* Fort Worth, TX: Harcourt Brace Jovanovich.

Awh, E. & Vogel, E. K. (2008). The bouncer in the brain. *Nature Neuroscience, New York, 11*(1), 5-6.

Baddeley, A. D. (1986). *Working memory.* Oxford: Oxford University Press II.

Barsalou, L. W. (1993). Flexibility, structure, and linguistic vagary in concepts: Manifestations of a compositional system of perceptual symbols. In Collins, A. F., Gathercole, S. E., Conway, M. A., Morris, P. E., (Eds.) *Theories of memory.* Hove, United Kingdom: Lawrence Erlbaum Associates.

Bartlett, J. C. (1977). Effects of immediate testing on delayed retrieval: Search and recovery operations with four types of cue. *Journal of Experimental Psychology: Human Learning and Memory, 3*(6), 719-732.

Begg, I. (1978). Similarity and contrast in memory for relations. *Memory and Cognition, 6*(5), 509-517.

Beilock, S. L., & Carr, T. H. (2001). On the fragility of skilled performance: What governs choking under pressure? *Journal of Experimental Psychology: General,130*(4). 701-725.

Beilock, S. L., Kulp, C. A., Holt, L. E., & Carr, T. H. (2004). More on the fragility of performance: Choking under pressure in mathematical problem solving. *Journal of Experimental Psychology: General, 133*(4), 584-600.

Bjork, R. A., & Whitten, W. B. (1974). Recency-sensitive retrieval processes in long-term free recall. *Cognitive Psychology, 6*(2), 173-189.Bransford, J. D., & Johnson, M. K. (1972). Contextual prerequisites for understanding: Some investigations of comprehension and recall. *Journal of Verbal Learning and Verbal Behavior, 11*(6), 717-726.

Bromley, S. (2006, October). *The end of math anxiety: Ensuring math success.* Presentation to the students of North Idaho College, Coeur d'Alene, ID.

Carpenter, S. K., Pashler, H., & Vul, E. (2006). What types of learning are enhanced by a cued recall test? *Psychonomic Bulletin & Review, Austin, 13*(5), 826-830.

Carpenter, S. K., Pashler, H. & Wixted, J. T. (2008). The effects of tests on learning and forgetting. *Memory & Cognition, Austin 36*(2), 438-448.

Chan, J. C. K., & McDermott, K. B. (2007). The testing effect in recognition memory: A dual process account. *Journal of Experimental Psychology: Learning, Memory and Cognition, 33*(2), 431-437.

Chan, J. C. K., McDermott, K. B. & Roediger, H. L. III. (2006). Retrieval-induced facilitation: Initially nontested material can benefit from prior testing of related material. *Journal of Experimental Psychology: General, 135*(4), 553-571.

Cohen, G., Kiss, G., & LeVoi, M. (1993). *Memory: Current issues.* Buckingham, United Kingdom: Open University Press.

Chase, C. I. (1983). Essay test scores and reading difficulty. *Journal of Educational Measurement, 20*(3), 293-297.

Craik, F. I. M., & Lockhart, R. S. (1972). Levels of processing: A framework for memory research. *Journal of Verbal Learning and Verbal Behavior,11*(6), 671-684.

Craik, F. I .M., & Tulving, E. (1975). Depth of processing and the relation of words in episodic memory. *Journal of Experimental Psychology: General, 104*(3), 268-294.

Crovitz, H. F., & Harvey, M. T. (1979). Visual imagery vs. semantic category as encoding conditions. *Bulletin of the Psychonomic Society, 13*(5), 291-292.

Dickinson, D. J., & O'Connell, D. Q. (1990). Effect of quality and quantity of study on student grades. *Journal of Educational Research, 83*(4), 227-231.Driskell, J. E., Willis, R. P., & Copper, C. (1992). Effect of over learning on retention. *Journal of Applied Psychology, 77*(5), 615-622.

Dunn, J. C., & Kirsner, K. (1989). Implicit memory: Task or process? In Lewandowsky, S., Dunn, J. C., & Kirsner, K. (Eds.), *Implicit memory: Theoretical issues.* Hillsdale, NJ: Lawrence Erlbaum Associates.

duNoüy, L. (1947). *Human Destiny.* New York: Longmans, Green & Co.

Einstein, G. O., & Hunt, R. R. (1980). Levels of processing and organization: Addictive effects of individual-item and relational processing. *Journal of Experimental Psychology: Human Learning and Memory, 6*(5), 588-598.

Ellis, H. C., & Hunt, R. R. (1993). *Fundamentals of cognitive psychology.* Madison, WI: Brown & Benchmark.

Epstein, M. L., Phillips, W. D., & Johnson, S. J. (1975). Recall of related and unrelated word pairs as a function of processing level. *Journal of Experimental Psychology: Human Learning and Memory, 1*(2), 149-152.

Erdelyi, M., Buschke, H., & Finkelstein, S. (1977). Hypermensia for Socratic stimuli: The growth of recall for an internally generated memory list abstracted from a series of riddles. *Memory and Cognition, 5*(3), 283-286.

Erdelyi, M. H., Finklestein, S., Herrell, N., Miller, B., & Thomas, J. (1976). Coding modality vs. input modality in hypermensia: Is a rose a rose a rose? *Cognition, 4*(4), 311-319.

Flannagan, D. A., & Blick, K. A. (1989). Levels of processing and the retention of word meanings. *Perceptual and Motor Skills, 68*(3, Pt. 2), 1123-1128.

Fletcher, C. R., & Bloom, C. P. (1988). Causal reasoning in the comprehension of simple narrative texts. *Journal of Memory and Language, 27*(3), 235-244.

Frankland, P. W. & Bontempi, B. (2005). The organization of recent and remote memories. *Nature Reviews: Neuroscience, London, 6*(2) 119-130.

Gambrall, L. B., & Jawitz, P. B. (1993). Mental imagery, text illustrations, and children's story comprehension and recall. *Reading Research Quarterly, 28*(3), 264-276.

Gardiner, J. M., & Java, R. I . (1993). Recognising and remembering. In Collins, A. F., Gathercole, S. E., Conway, M. A., Morris, P. E., (Eds.). *Theories of memory.* Hove, United Kingdom: Lawrence Erlbaum Associates.

Glass, D. C., & Singer, J. E. (1972). E*xperiments on noise & social stressors.* New York: Academic Press.

Glen, D. (2007). You will be tested on this. *Chronicle of Higher Education,* http://chronicle.com/weekly/v53/i40/40a01401.htm

Goldstein, E. B. (2011). *Cognitive psychology.* Belmont, CA: Wadsworth.

Graf, P., & Schacter, D. (1985). Implicit and explicit memory for new associations in normal and amnesic subjects. *Journal of Experimental Psychology: Learning, Memory, and Cognition, 11*(3), 501-518.

Greene, R. L. (1992). *Human memory: Paradigms and paradoxes.* Hillsdale, NJ: Lawrence Erlbaum Associates.

Greenwald, A. G., & Banaji, M. R. (1989). The self as a memory system: Powerful, but ordinary. *Journal of Personality and Social Psychology, 57*(1), 41-54.

Huber, R., Ghilardi, M. F., Massimini, M., & Tononi, G. (2004). Local sleep and learning. *Nature, London 430*(6995), 78-81.

Hunt, R. R., & Einstein, G. O. (1981). Relational item-specific information in memory. *Journal of Verbal Learning and Verbal Behavior, 20*(5), 497-514.

Hunt, R. R., & McDaniel, M. A. (1993). The enigma of organization and distinctiveness. *Journal of Memory and Language, 32*(4), 421-445.

Hunt, R. R., & Seta, C. E. (1993). Category size effects in recall: The roles of individual item and relational information. *Journal of Experimental Psychology: Learning, Memory, and Cognition, 10*(3), 454-464.

Karni, A., Tanne, D., Rubenstein, B. S., Askenasy, J. J. M., et al. (1994). Dependence on REM sleep of overnight improvement of a perceptual skill. *Science, 265*(5172), 679-682.

Kardash, C. A., Royer, J. M., & Greene, B. A. (1988). Effects of schemata on both encoding and retrieval of information from prose. *Journal of Educational Psychology, 80*(3), 324-329.

Karpicke, J. D., Butler, A. C., & Roediger, H. L. III. (2009). Metacognitive strategies in student learning: Do students practice retrieval when they study on their own? *Memory, 17,* 471-479.

Karpicke, J. D., & Roediger, H. L. III. (2010). Is expanding retrieval a superior method for learning text materials? *Memory & Cognition. Austin, 38*(1), 116-124.

Kendzierski, D. (1980). Self-schemata and scripts: The recall of self-referent and scriptal information. *Personality and Social Psychology Bulletin, 6*(1), 23-29.

Klassen, J. B. (2016, March). *The end of math anxiety: Ensuring math success.* Presentation to the students of North Idaho College, Coeur d'Alene, ID.

Klassen, K. T. (1995). *The effect of spelling errors on subjective evaluation of both college level essays and the character of their authors.* Unpublished master's thesis, Eastern Washington University.

Klein, S. B., Loftus, J., Kihlsteom, J. F., & Aseron, R. (1989). Effects of item specific and relational information on hypermensic recall. *Journal of Experimental Psychology: Learning, Memory, and Cognition, 15*(6), 1192-1197.

Kornell N., & Son, L. K. (2009). Learners' choices and beliefs about self-testing. *Memory 17,* 493-501.

Kosslyn, S. M. (1980). *Image and mind.* Cambridge, MA: Harvard University Press.

Lakoff, G. & Nunez, R. E. (2000). *Where mathematics comes from.* New York: Basic Books.

Lazarus, R. S., & Folkman, S. (1984). *Stress, Appraisal and Coping.* New York: Springer.

Mantyla, T. (1986). Optimizing cue effectiveness: Recall of 500 and 600 incidentally learned words. *Journal of Experimental Psychology: Learning, Memory, and Cognition, 12*(1), 303-312.

Mantyla, T., & Nilsson, L. G. (1988). Cue distinctiveness and forgetting: Effectiveness of self-generated cues in delayed recall. *Journal of Experimental Psychology: Learning, Memory, and Cognition, 14*(3), 502-529.

Maquet, P., Laureys, P. P., Peigneux, P., et al. (2000). Experience-dependent changes in cerebral activation during human REM sleep. *Nature Neuroscience, New York, 3*(8), 831-836.

Marsh, E. J., Roediger, H. L. III., Bjork, R. A., & Bjork, E. L. (2007). The memorial consequences of multiple choice testing. *Psychonomic Bulletin and Review, 14*(2), 194-199.

McDaniel, M. A., Anderson, J. L., Derbish, M. H., & Morrisette, N. (2007). Testing the testing effect in the classroom. *European Journal of Cognitive Psychology, 19,* 494-513.

Menke, D. J., & Pressley, M. (1994). Elaborative interrogation: Using "why" questions to enhance the learning from text. *Journal of Reading, 37*(8), 642-645.

Murphy, M. D., & Wallace, W. P. (1974). Encoding specificity: Semantic change between storage and retrieval cues. *Journal of Experimental Psychology, 103*(4), 768-774.

Myers, D. G. (2010). *Psychology 9e.* New York: Worth Publishers.

Nadel, L, & Muscovitch, M. (1997). Memory consolidation, retrograde amnesia and the hippocampal complex. *Current Opinion in Neurobiology*, 7, 217-227.

Parkin, A. J. (1993). *Memory: Phenomena, experiment, and theory.* Oxford: Blackwell Publishers.

Pashler, H., Rohrer, D., Cepeda, N. J., & Carpenter, S. K. (2007). Enhancing learning and retarding forgetting: Choices and consequences. *Psychonomic Bulletin & Review, Austin, 14*(2), 187-193.

Payne, D. G., Roediger, H. L. III. (1987). Hypermensia occurs in recall but not recognition. *The American Journal of Psychology. Urbana, 100*(2), 145.

Peigneux, P., Laureys, S., Fuchs, S., et al. (2004). Are spatial memories strengthened in the human hippocampus during slow wave sleep? *Neuron, 44,* 535-545.

Pellegrino, J. W., & Battig, W. F. (1972). Effects of semantic list structure differences in free recall. *Psychonomic Science, 29*(2), 65-67.

Penney, C. G. (1988). A beneficial effect of part-list cueing with unrelated words. *Bulletin of the Psychonomic Society, 26*(4), 297-300.

Reddy, B. G., & Bellezza, F. S. (1983). Encoding specificity in free recall. *Journal of Experimental Psychology: Learning, Memory, and Cognition, 9*(1), 167-174.

Robins, S., & Mayer, R. E. (1993). Schema training in analogical reasoning. *Journal of Educational Psychology, 85*(3), 529-538.

Roediger, H. L., & Thorpe, L. A. (1978). The role of recall time in producing hypermensia. *Memory and Cognition, 6*(3), 296-305.

Roediger, H. L. III (1990). Implicit memory: A commentary. *Bulletin of the Psychonomic Society, 28*(4), 373-380.

Roediger, H. L. III, Weldon, M. S., & Challis, B. H. (1989). Explaining dissociations between implicit and explicit measures of retention: A processing account. In H. L. Roediger III, & F. I. M. Craik (Eds.) *Varieties of memory and consciousness: Essays in honor of Endel Tulvig.* Hillsdale, NJ: Lawrence Erlbaum Associates Inc.

Rose, R. J. (1992). Degree of learning, interpolated tests, and rate of forgetting. *Memory and Cognition, 20*(6), 621-632.

Rybash, J. M., & Osborne, J. L. (1991). Implicit memory, the serial position effect, and test awareness. *Bulletin of the Psychonomic Society, 29*(4),327-330.

Salz, E., & Dixon, D. (1982). Let's pretend: The role of motoric imagery in memory for sentences and words. *Journal of Experimental Child Psychology, 43*(1), 77-92.

Schneider, W. (1993). Domain-specific knowledge and memory performance in children. *Educational Psychology Review, 5*(3), 257-273.

Seifert, T. L. (1993). Effects of elaborative interrogation with prose passages. *Journal of Educational Psychology, 85*(4), 642-651.

Semb, G. B., Ellis, J. A., & Araujo, J. (1993). Long-term memory for knowledge learned in school. *Journal of Educational Psychology, 85*(2), 305-316.

Seligman, M. E., & Binik, Y. M., (1977). The safety signal hypothesis. In H. Davis & H. Hurwitz (Eds.) *Pavlovian interactions.* Hillsdale, NJ: Erlbaum.

Smith, C., & Lapp, L. (1991). Increases in number of REMs and REM density in humans following an itensive learning period. *Sleep, 14*(4), 325-330.

Smith, C., & MacNeill, C. (1993). A paradoxical sleep-dependent window for memory 53-56 h. after the end of avoidance training. *Psychobiology, 21*(2), 109-112.

Smith, S. M. (1982). Enhancement of recall using multiple environmental contexts during learning. *Memory and Cognition, 10* (5), 405-412.

Takata, S. (1994). The guided essay examination for sociology and other courses. *Teaching Sociology, 22*(2), 189-194.

Tilley, A. J. (1981). Retention over a period of REM or non-REM sleep. *British Journal of Psychology, 72*(2), 241-248.

Treisman, A. M., & Gelade, G. (1980). A feature integration theory of attention. *Cognitive Psychology, 12*(1), 97-136.

Tulving, E. (1985). How many memory systems are there? *American Psychologist, 40*(4), 385-398.

Vogel, E. K., McCullough, A. W., & Machizawa, M. G. (2005). Neural measures reveal individual differences in controlling access to working memory. *Nature. London, 438*(7067), 500-503.

Weldon, M. S., & Roediger, H. L. (1987). Altering retrieval demands reverses the picture superiority effect. *Memory and Cognition, 15*(4), 269-280.

Wood, E., Willoughby, T., Kaspar, V., & Idle, T. (1994). Enhancing adolescents' recall of factual content: The impact of provided versus self-generated elaborations. *The Alberta Journal of Educational Research, 40*(1), 57-65.

Wright, A. A., Cook, R. G., Rivera, J. J., Shyan, M. R., Neiworth, J. J., & Jitsumori, M. (1990). Naming, rehearsal, and interstimulus interval effects in memory processing. *Journal of Experimental Psychology: Learning, Memory and Cognition, 16*(6), 1043-1059.

Yekovich, F. R., & Thorndyke, P. W. (1981). An evaluation of alternative functional models of narrative schemata. *Journal of Verbal Learning and Verbal Behavior, 20*(4), 454-469.